The Super Saxophone

Music Theory Book 1

A theory book especially for saxophone players

All the basics to get you going.
Easy to follow explanations,
puzzles and more.
All with the beginner saxophone player in mind.

Amanda Oosthuizen

Jemima Oosthuizen

The Super Saxophone Series
Wild Music Publications
www.wildmusicpublications.com

We hope you enjoy *The Super Saxophone Music Theory Book 1.*

Take a look at our other exciting books, including: 50+ Greatest Classics, Catch the Beat, Christmas Duets, Easy Tunes from Around the World, Trick or Treat – A Halloween Suite, Champagne and Chocolate, Fish 'n' Ships, and many more solo and duet books.

For more info on other amazing books, please go to:

WildMusicPublications.com

Visit our secret page for a **free backing track,**
and more fun things for free! visit:

http://WildMusicPublications.com/**7secret-saxophone9-tracks/**

And use the password: **Ben.D.Sax.**

Happy Music Making!

The Wild Music Publications Team

To keep up -to-date with our new releases, why not **follow us on Twitter**

@WMPublications

To play the Saxophone well, you need to read music and understand the mysteries of music theory. The Super Saxophone Music Theory Book 1 includes all the basics you'll need up to Grade 2 Saxophone and is written with the beginner saxophone player in mind. Take it slowly, complete a little bit at a time and have fun!

Each section explains a new aspect of music in an easy-to-read way and is followed by exercises and puzzles to help you remember what you've learnt.

 Writing activities are shown by a saxophone pencil.

After several sections, you will find a Check page where you can see how much you have remembered and keep score.

At the end of the book, there are Saxophone information pages, more puzzles, a list of musical terms and symbols and a chart where you can keep a record of the sections you have completed.

If you want to check your **ANSWERS**, a free answer book download is available on the **SECRET SAXOPHONE PAGE** of our website. Find out how to get there on the second page of the book.

When you have finished, take a look at Book 2. It includes all the crazy theory you need to know from Grades 3 – 5 Saxophone including: ornaments, more Saxophone facts, making scales, compound time signatures and much more.

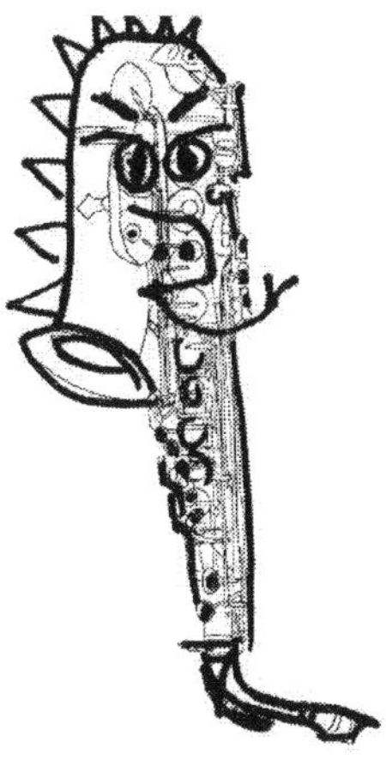

Contents

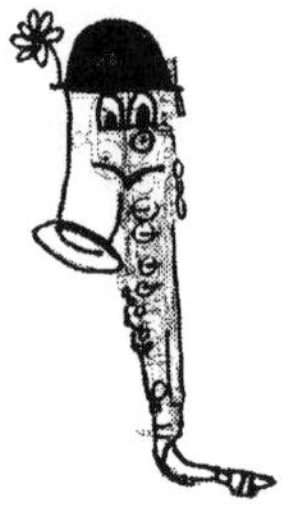

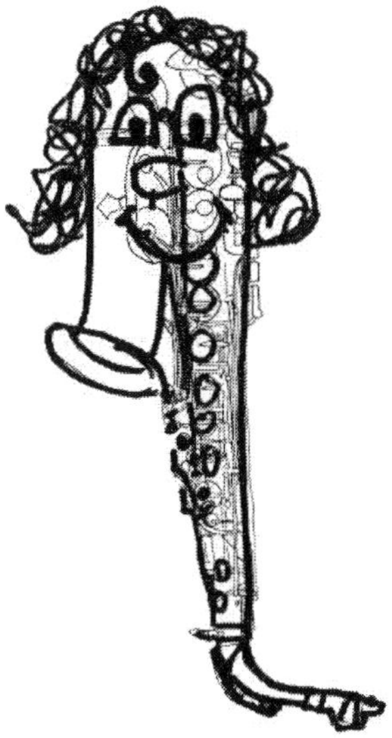

Treble Clef

Saxophone music is written in treble clef. Treble clef is also called G clef.

Music is written on five lines called a staff or stave. The treble clef is drawn at the start of every staff.

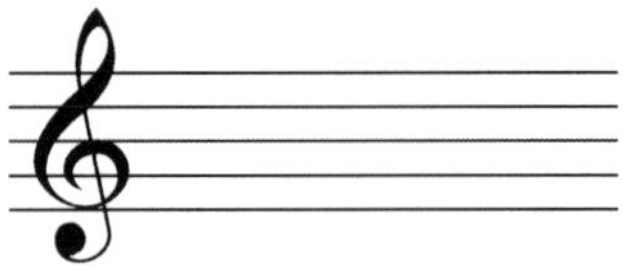

Staff

Draw a treble clef in every measure. It may help to start by curling around a dot on the second line.

Music is divided into bar measures by bar lines.

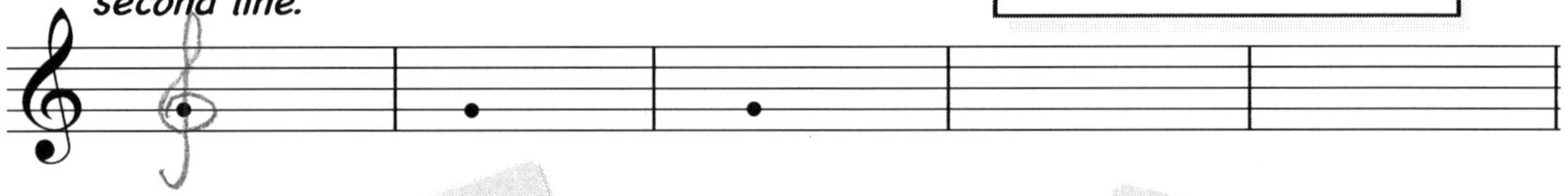

The end of a section of music is shown by a double bar line.

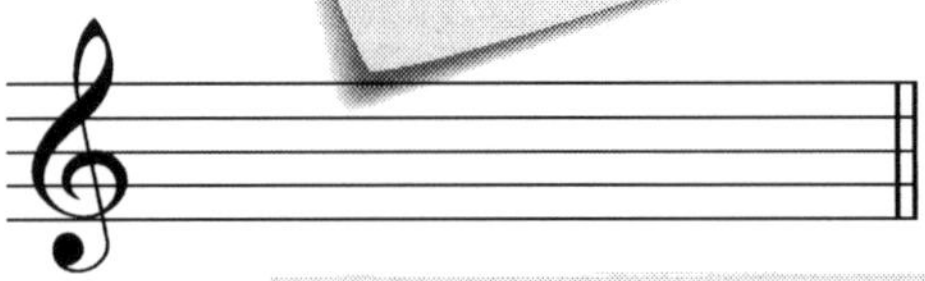

The end of a piece of music is shown by a final bar line.

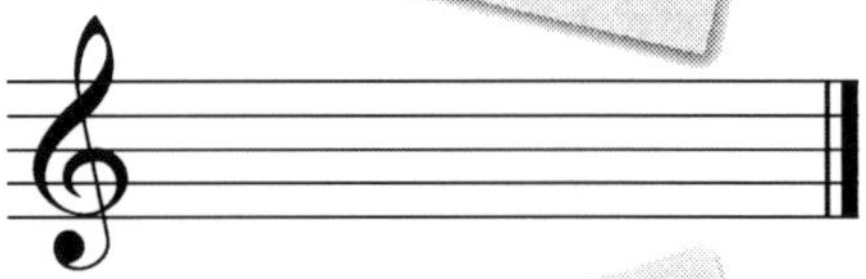

A phrase is a short section of music that makes sense, rather like a sentence.

Phrases are shown by a large slur.

Phrases are often four measures long.

Phrase

Letter Names

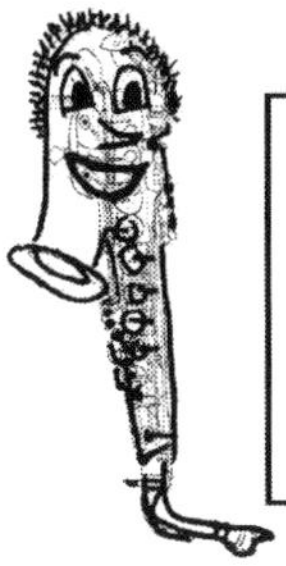

Notes are written on the lines and in the spaces.

The lower sounds are at the bottom of the staff.

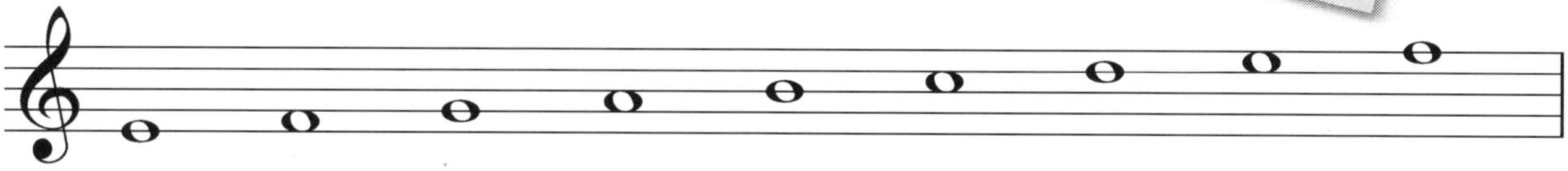

E F G A B C D E F

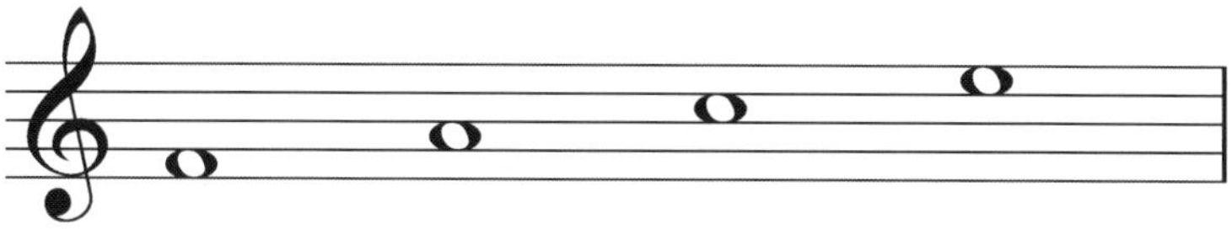

F A C E

Notes in the spaces spell FACE

Write the letter names under these notes.

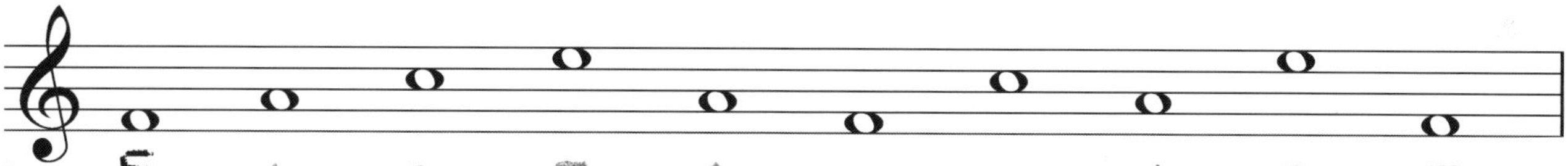

F (example) A C E A F C A E F

Write these notes in the spaces.

F A C E

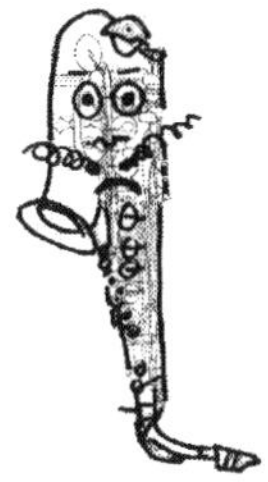

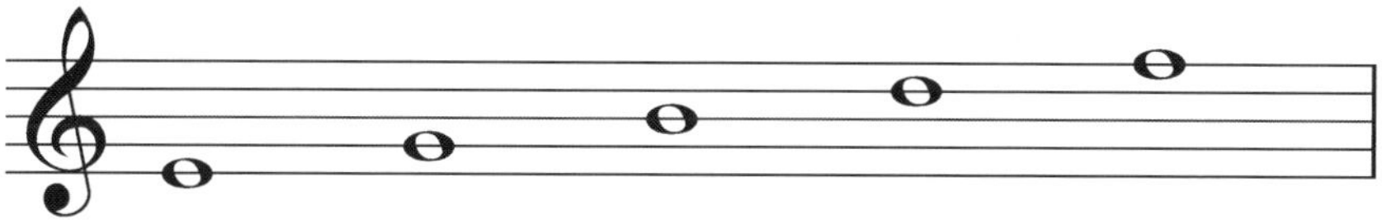

E G B D F

Every Good Boy Deserves Football

Notes on the lines

Write the letter names under these notes.

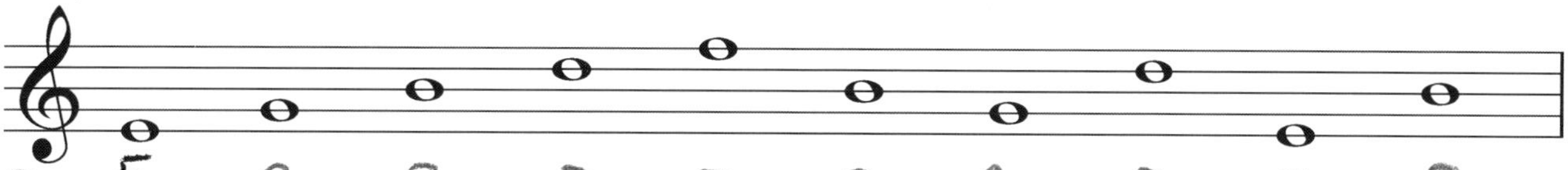

E (example) G B D F B G D E B

Write your own selection of notes on the lines.

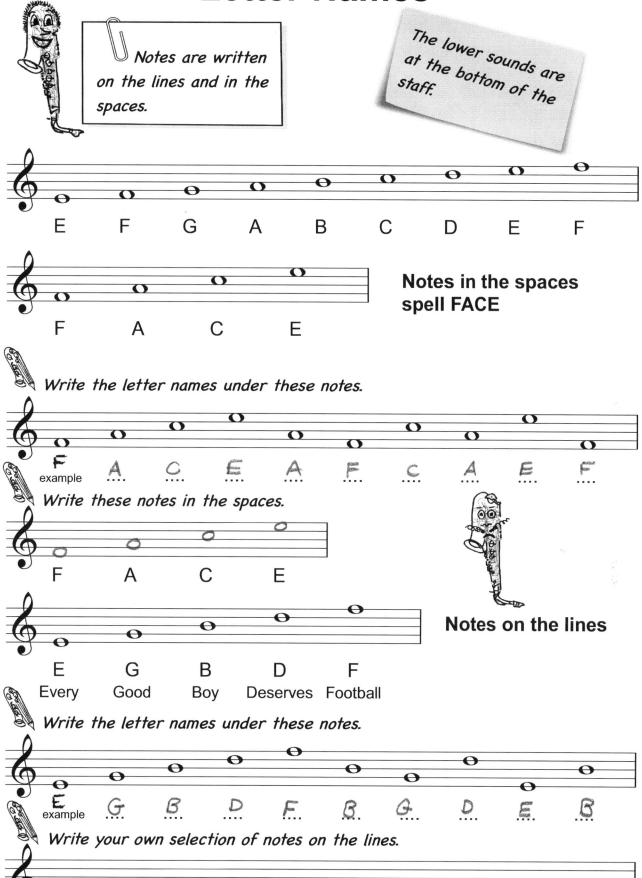

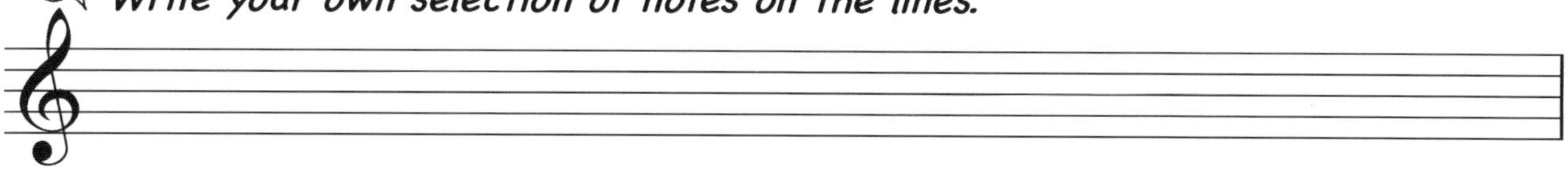

Write the letter names under these notes in the spaces.

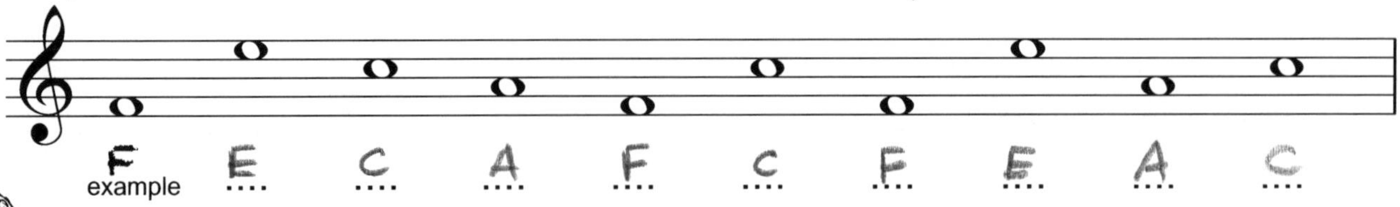

Write the letter names under these notes on the lines.

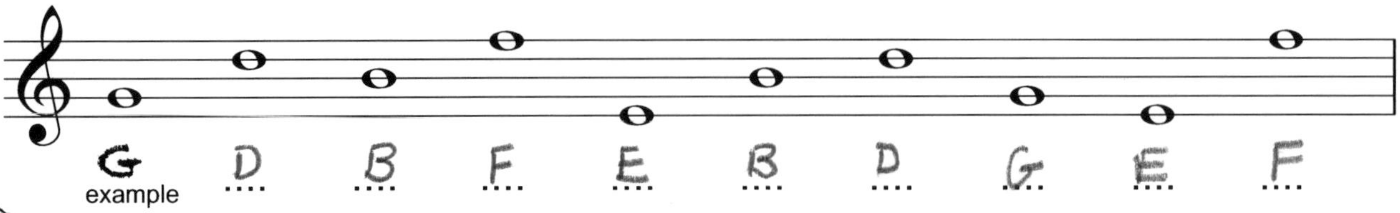

Write your own selection of notes on lines and in spaces.

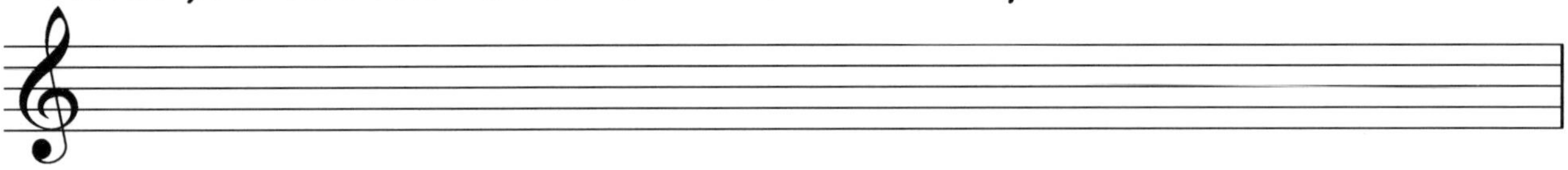

Write the letter names under these notes on lines and in spaces.

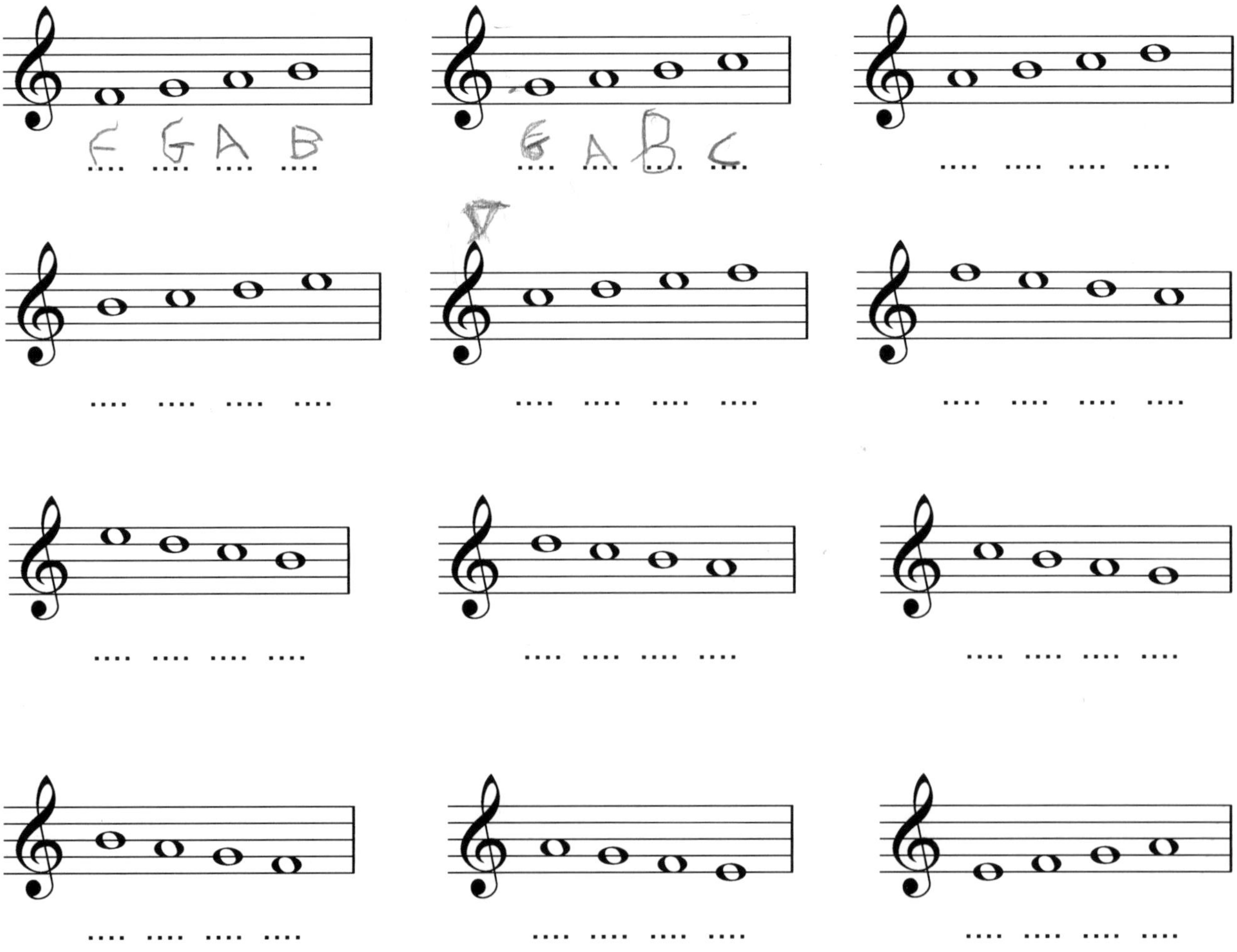

Write the notes in spaces above the letter names.

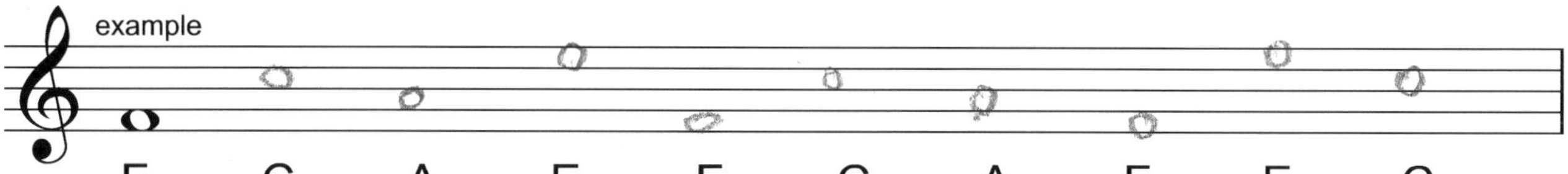

F C A E F C A F E C

Write the notes on lines above the letter names.

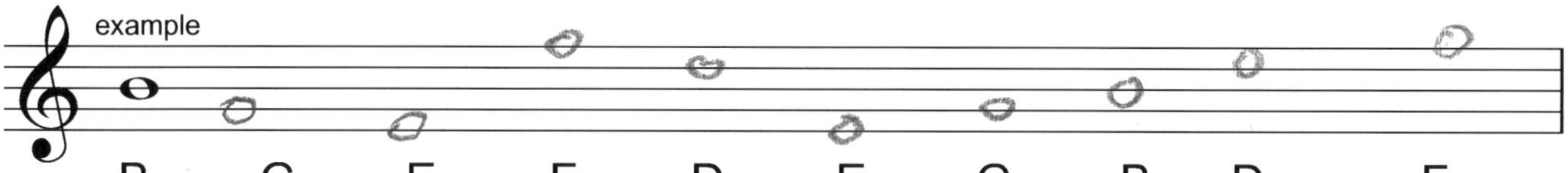

B G E F D E G B D F

Write the notes on lines or spaces above the letter names.

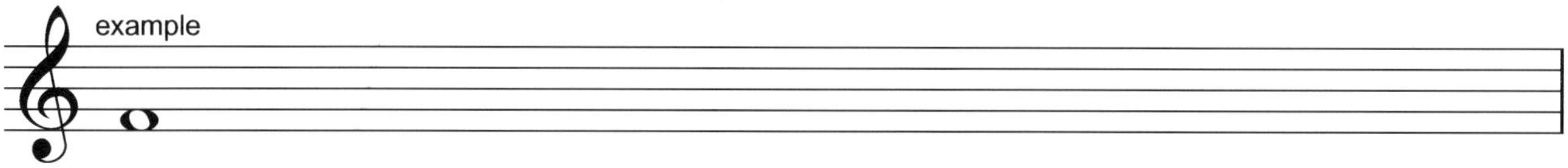

F G A B B C D E E D C B

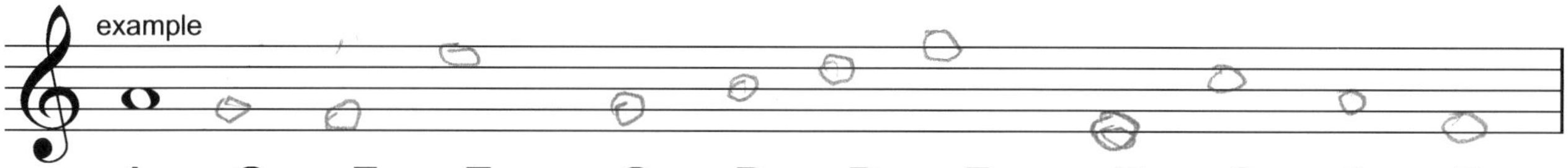

A G F E G B D F E C A F

Write notes in lines and spaces starting from the bottom of the staff.

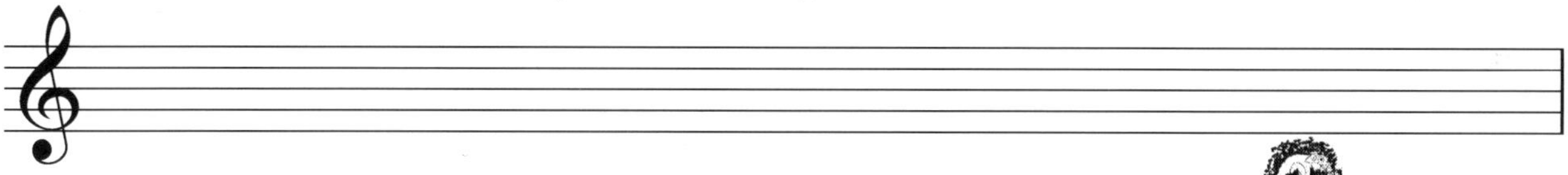

Write the letter names beneath the notes.

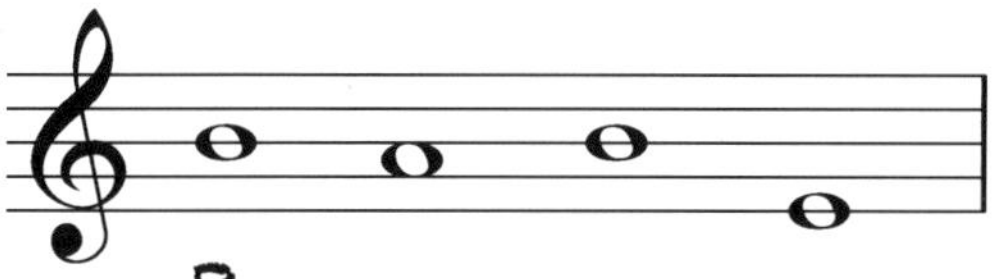

B
example ....

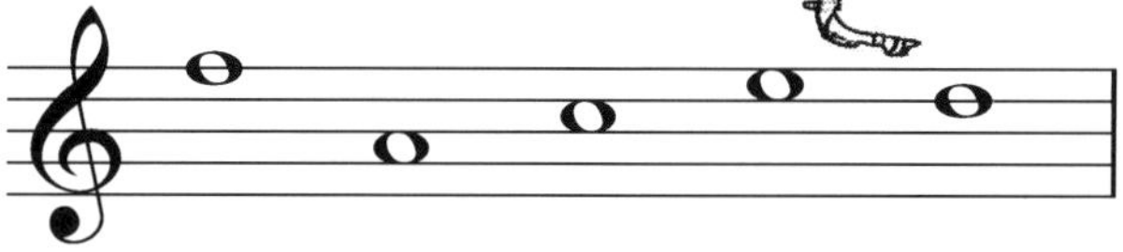

....

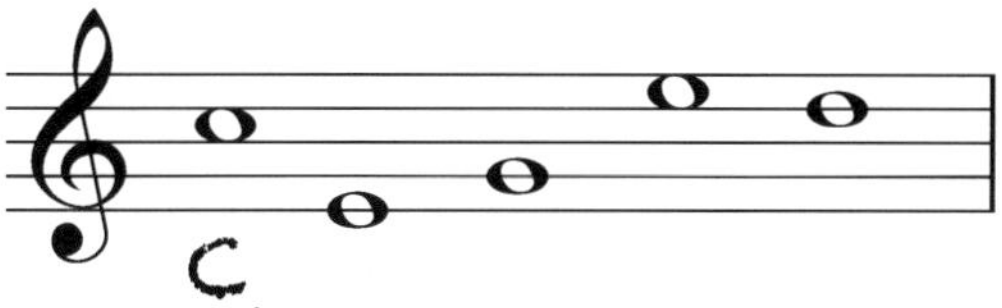

C
example ....

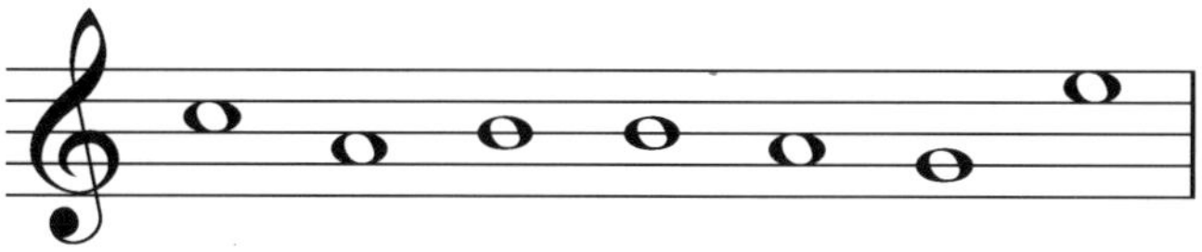

....

Write these words in music.

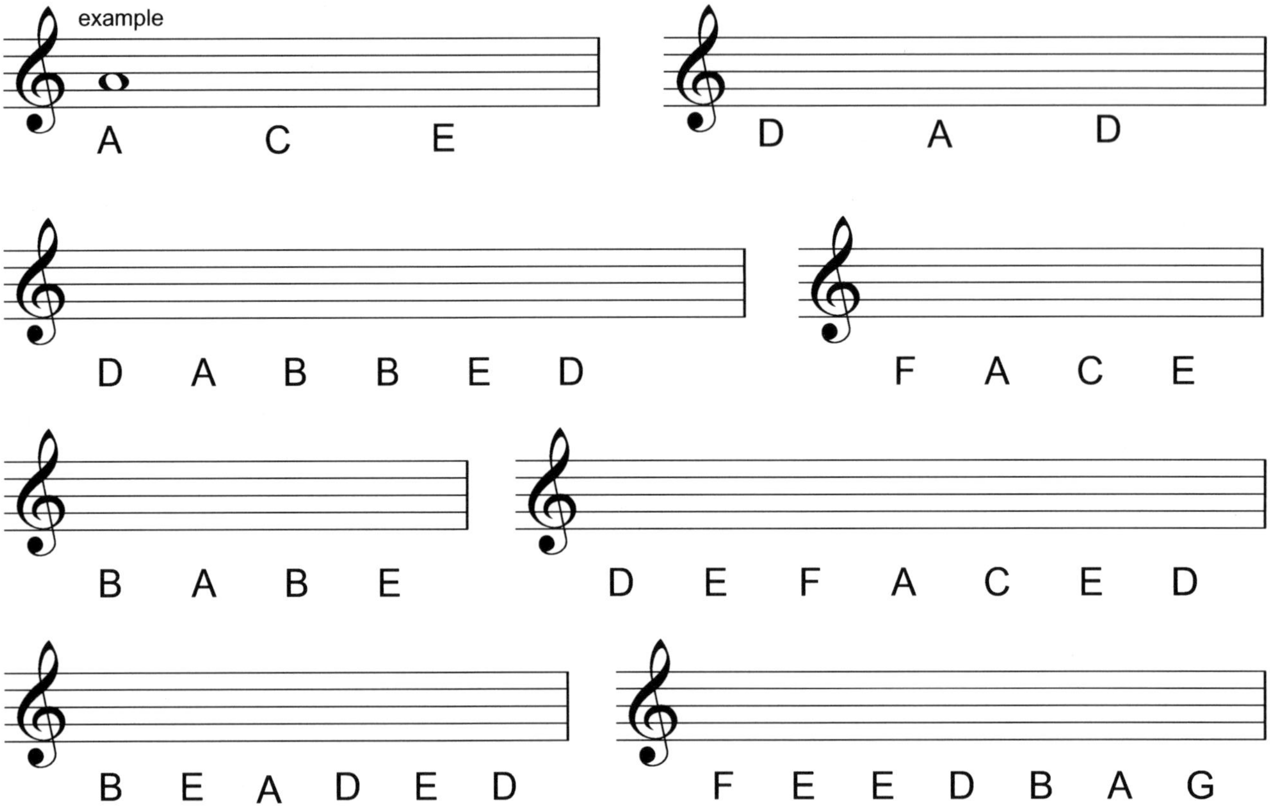
example
A C E
D A D
D A B B E D
F A C E
B A B E
D E F A C E D
B E A D E D
F E E D B A G

Write the letter names under the notes.

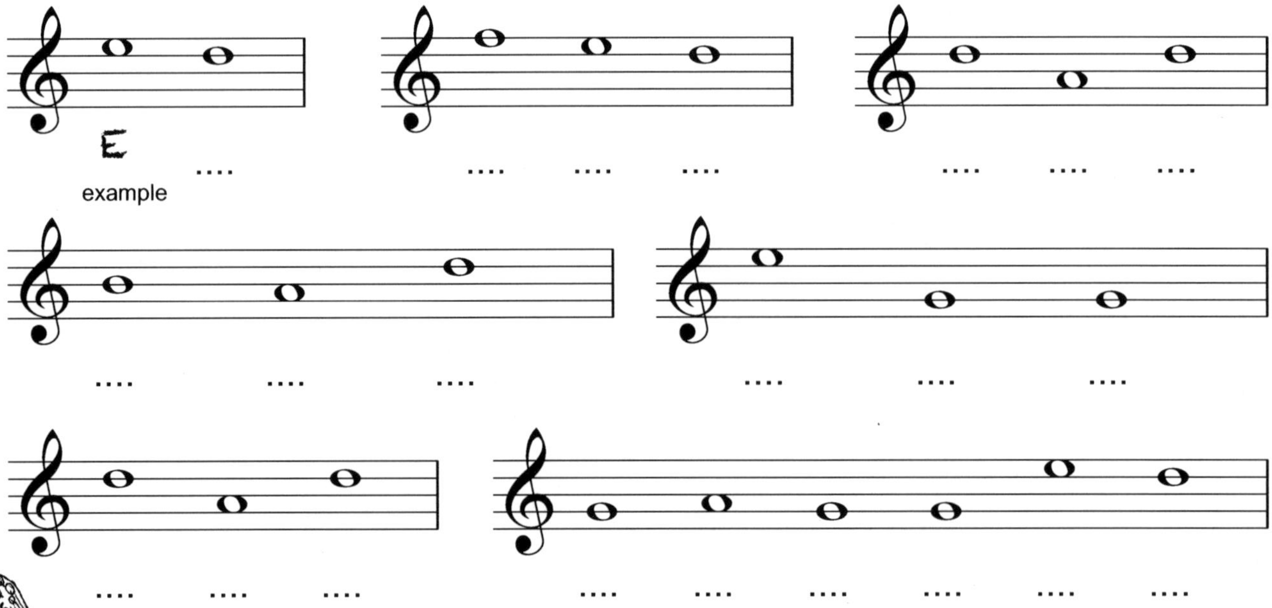
E
example

Write a phrase of music beginning and ending on C.

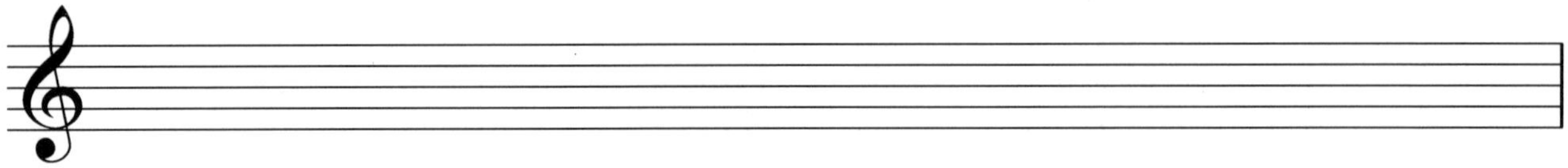

o - whole note - semibreve.
d - half note - minim
d - quarter note - crotchet

Note Values

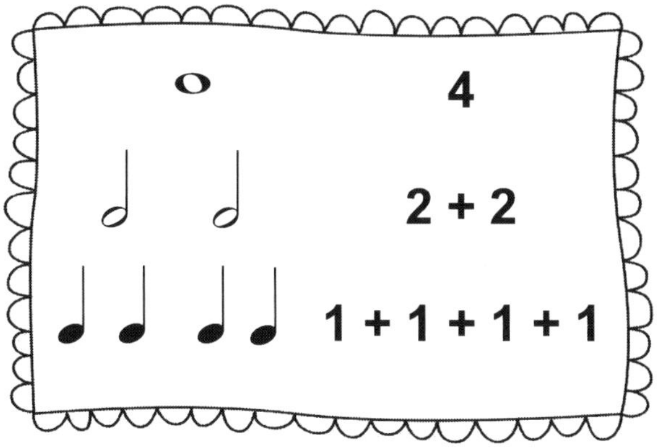

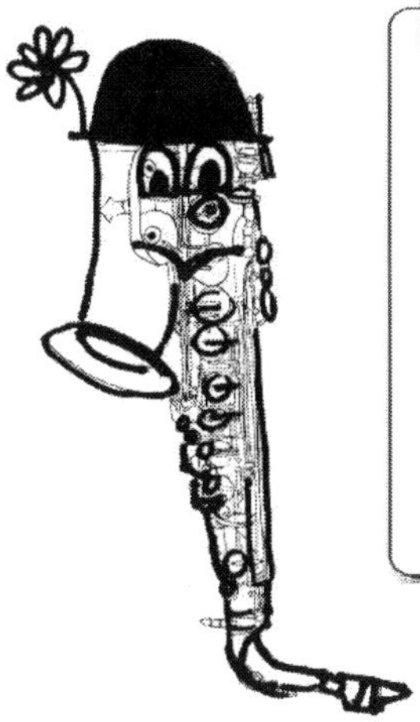

Dotted Notes

A dot next to a note adds half its value to that note.

Whole note - 4 counts

Write a wholel note in every measure.

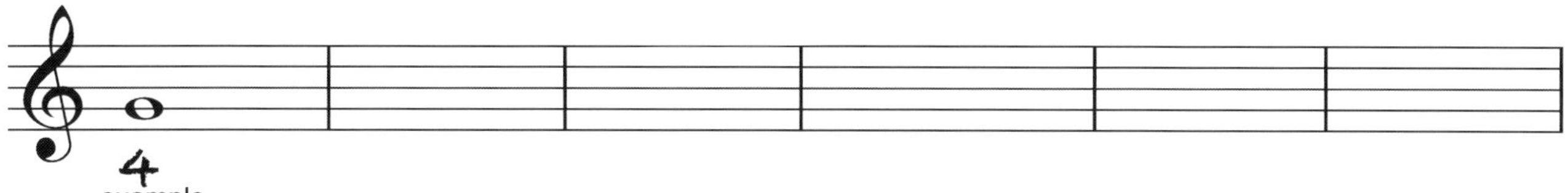

4
example ....

Dotted half note - 3 counts

Write a dotted half note in every measure.

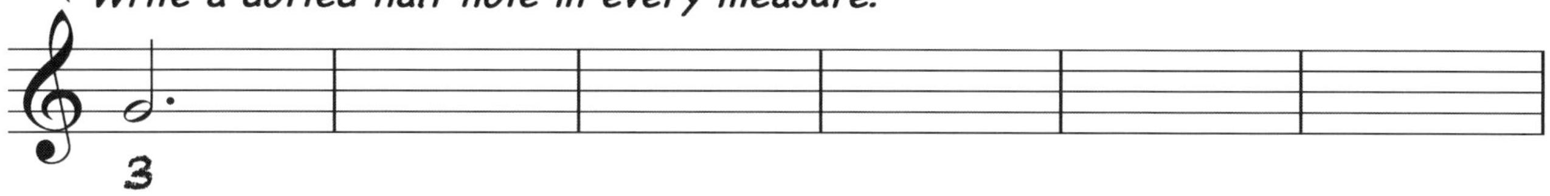

3
example ....

Half note - 2 counts

Write a half note in every measure.

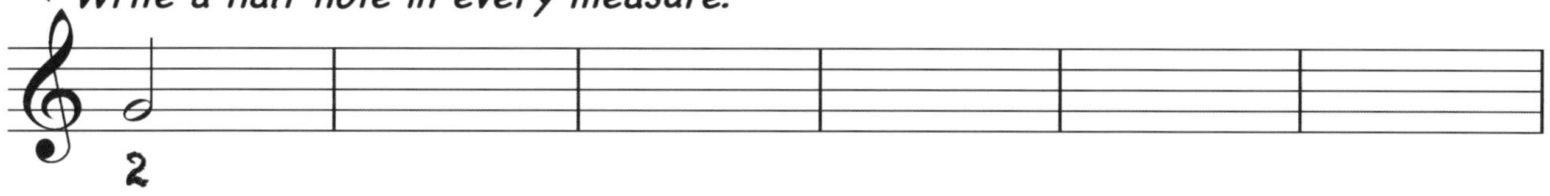

2
example ....

Quarter note - 1 count

Write a quarter note in every measure.

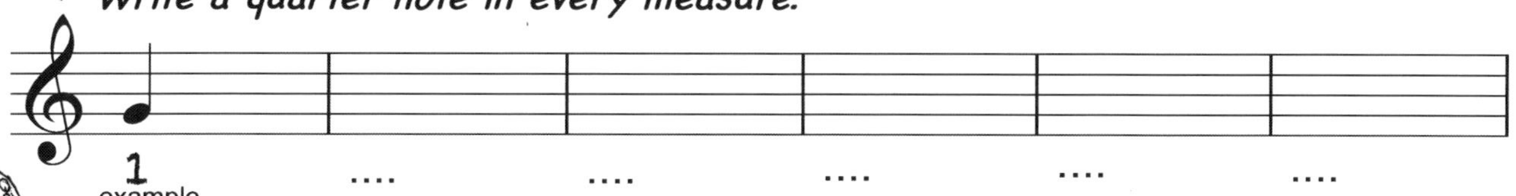

1
example ....

Write a mixed selection of note values on the notes G and A.

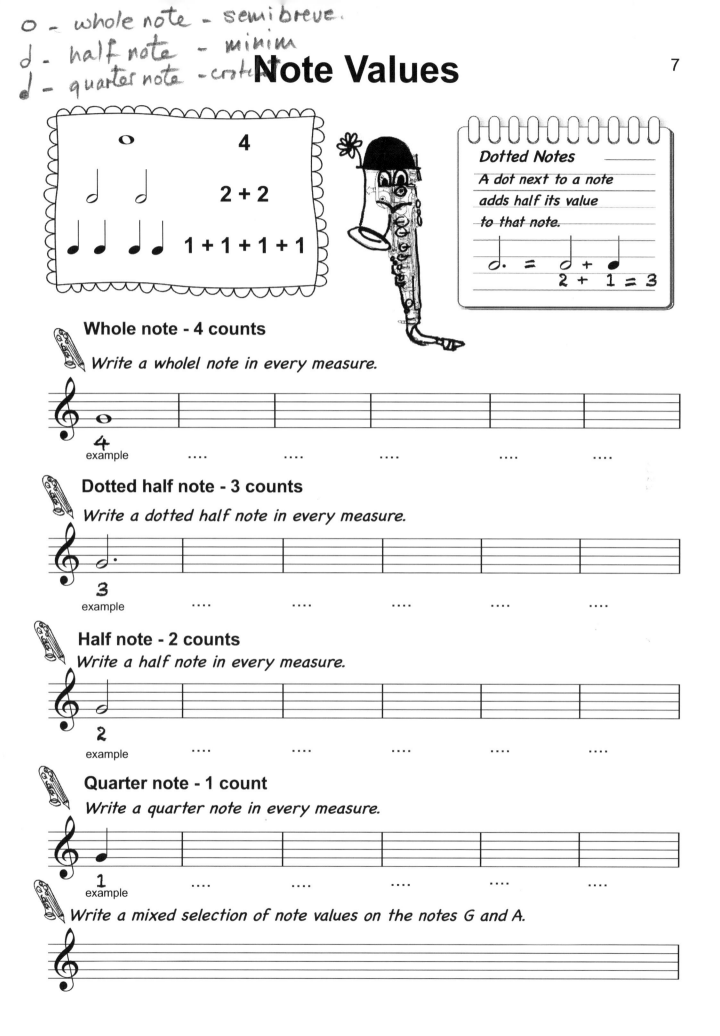

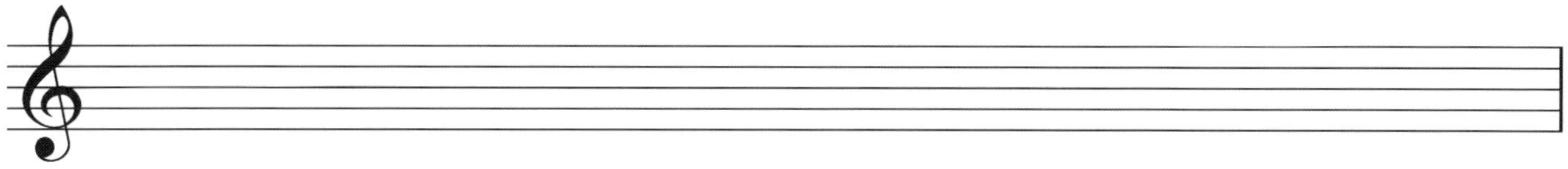

8 Write the number of counts.

♩ ♩ ♩ o ♩. ♩ ♩ o ♩. ♩ o ♩. ♩

2   1 4 3 2 1 4 3 1 4 3 2
example ....

Ties
A tie is a loop joining notes
that are the same. It means
add the notes together.

♩ ‿ ♩. = 2 + 3

Write the counts and do the sum.

2 + 1 = 3
.... example ....

2 + 2 = 4
....

.... + ... = 3

.... + ... + ... = 6

.... + ... + ... = 7

.... + ... = 4

.... + ... = 7

Write the missing notes below the *.

*
3 counts

*
9 counts

*
5 counts

Write notes that make each measure add up to four quarter notes.

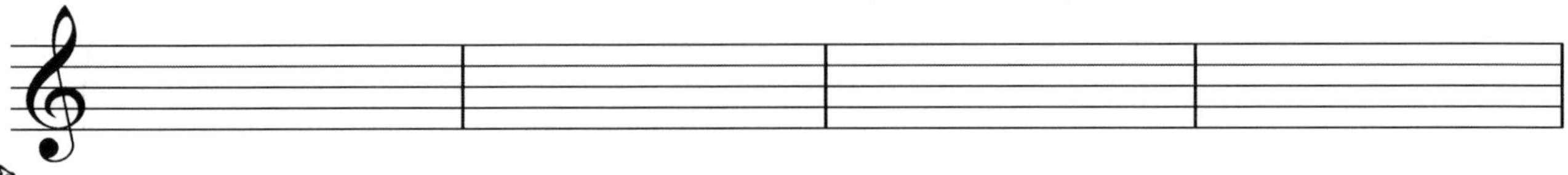

Write notes that make each measure add up to three quarter notes.

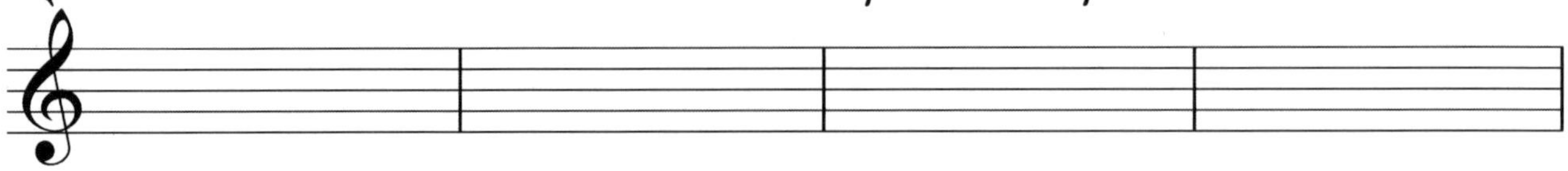

Using G, A, B and C, write notes of different lengths.

Match the boxes with the correct number of counts.

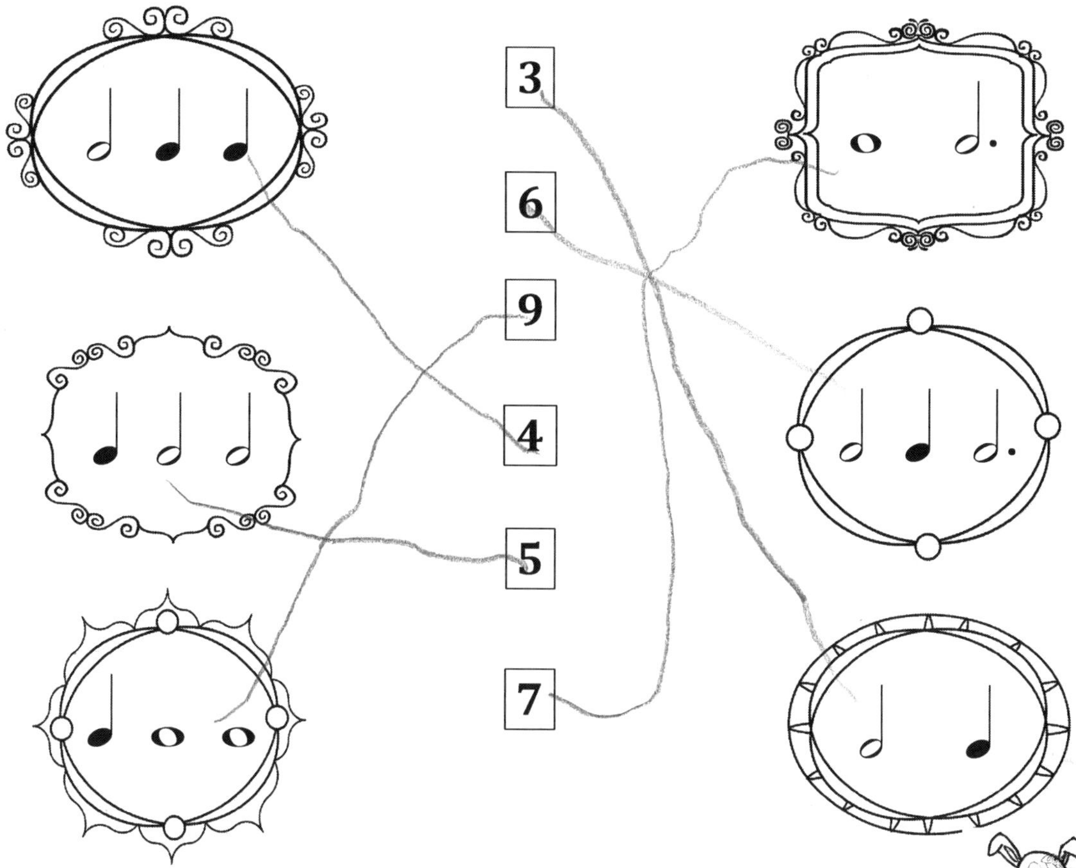

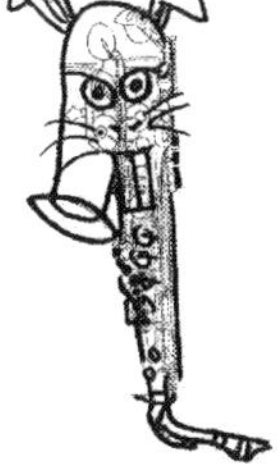

Copy this music exactly.

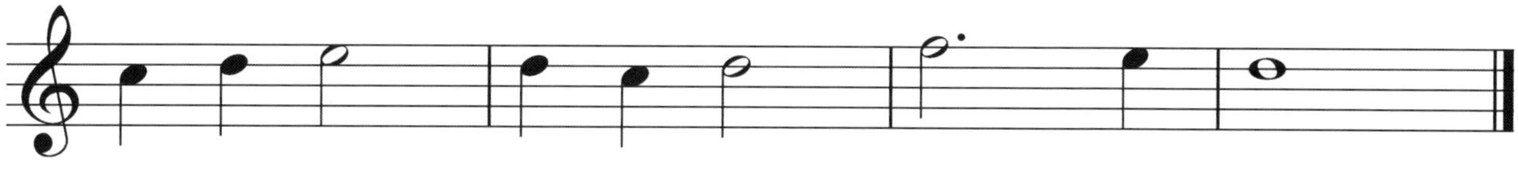

Stems

The stems are on the left when they go down.

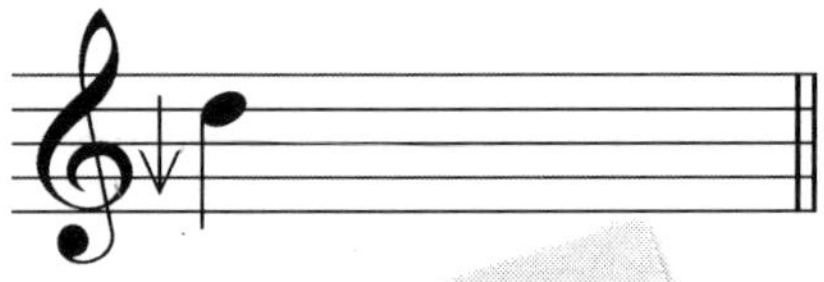

All notes except whole notes have stems.

The stems are on the right when they go up.

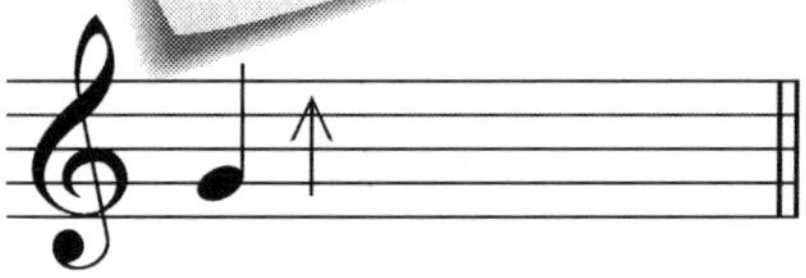

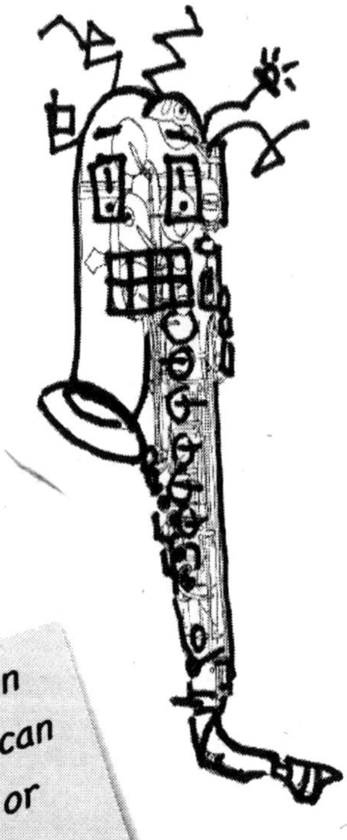

The stem goes down if a note is above the middle line.

The stem goes up if a note is below the middle line.

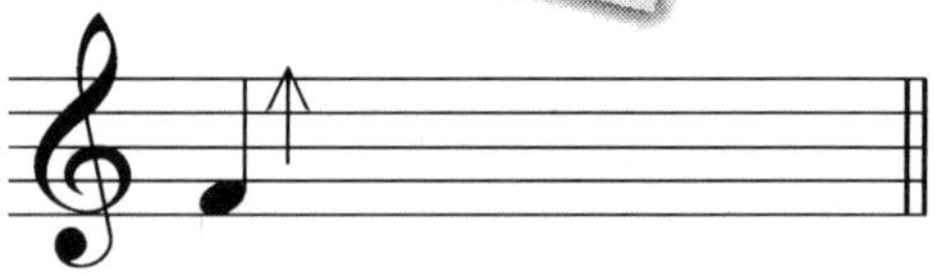

The stem of B on the middle line can go either up or down.

Add a stem to each of these noteheads.

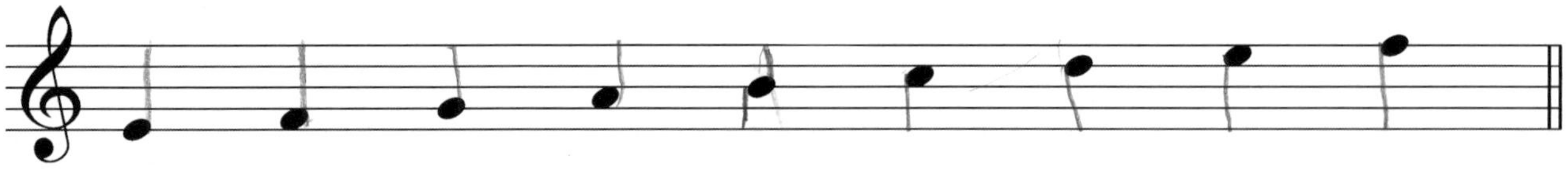

Write a mixture of low and high noteheads and then add the stems.

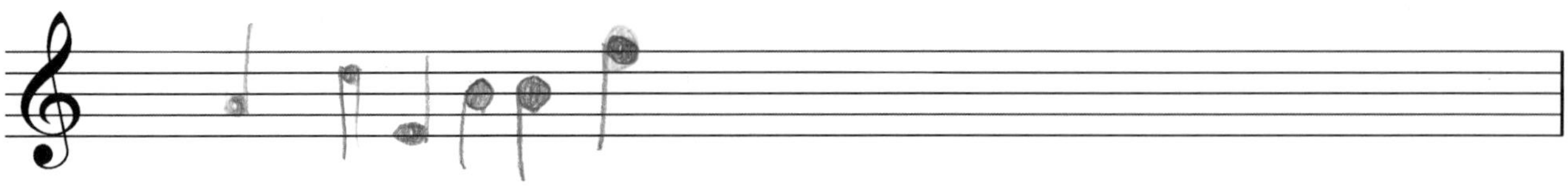

Rests

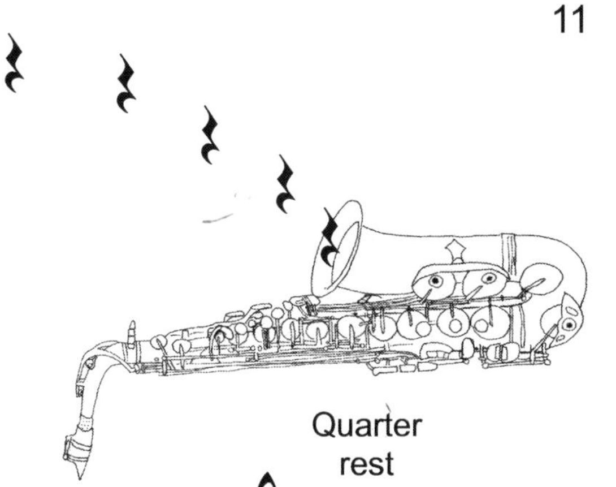

Rests show silence instead of notes.

Whole rest

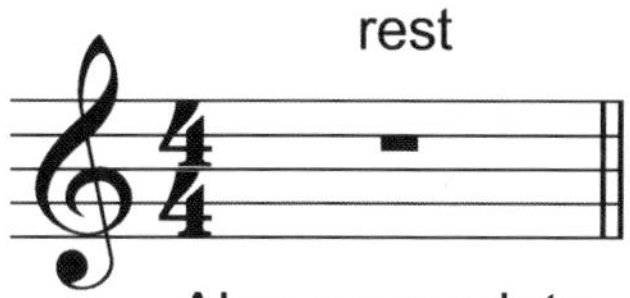

Also a complete measure's rest

Half rest

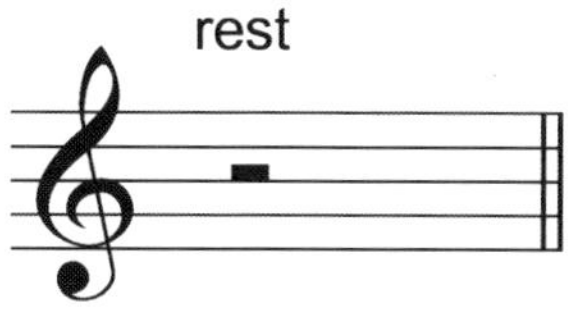

Quarter rest

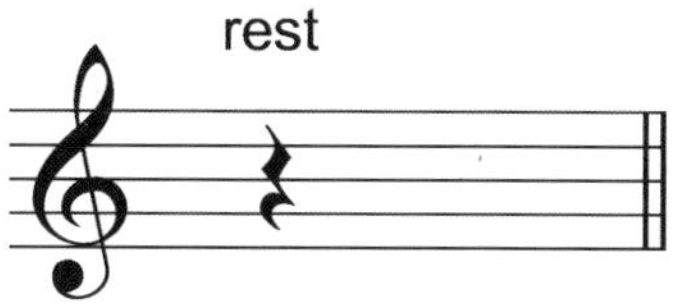

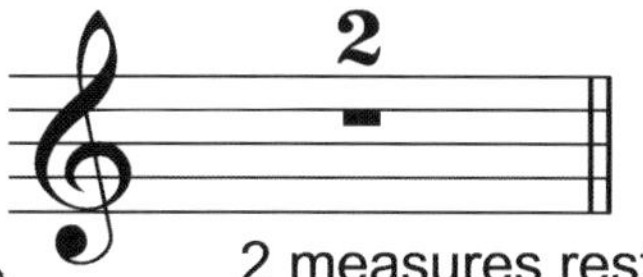

2 measures rest

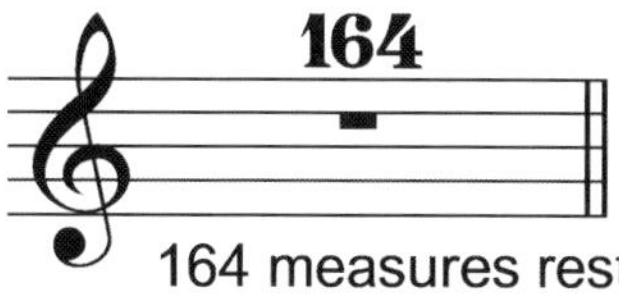

164 measures rest

Dotted half rest

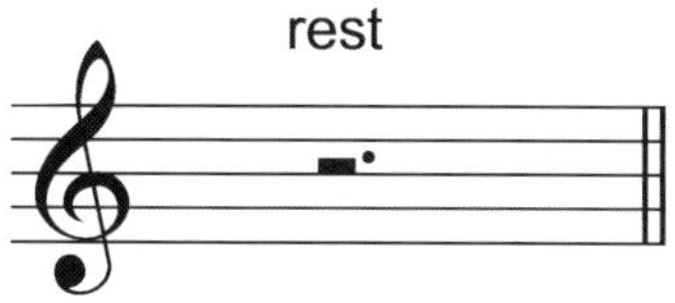

Match the boxes with the correct number of counts.

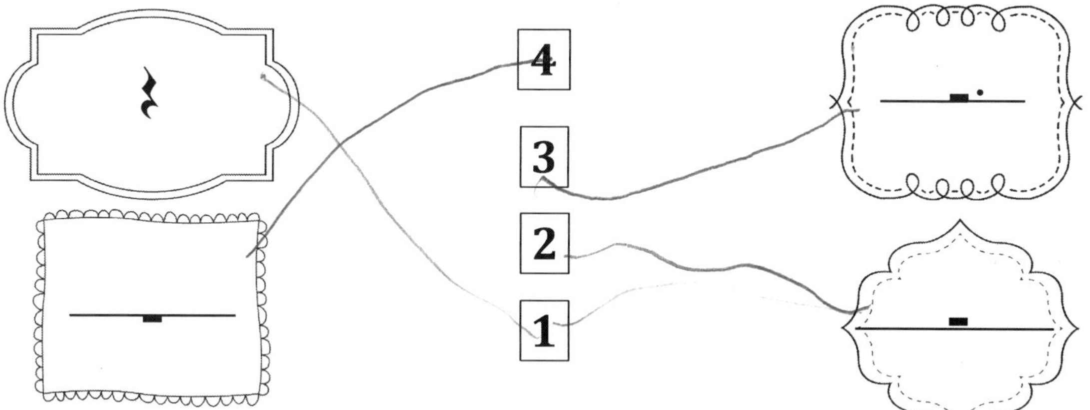

Draw the rest to match the note.

Draw in the rests that make every measure add up to four.

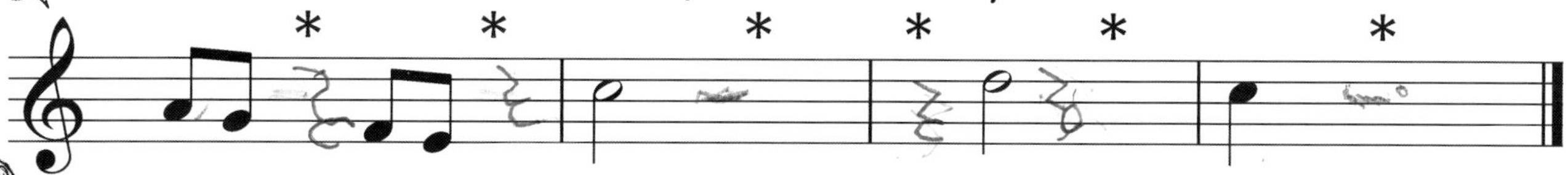

Fill every measure with notes and rests that add up to three, and then play them!

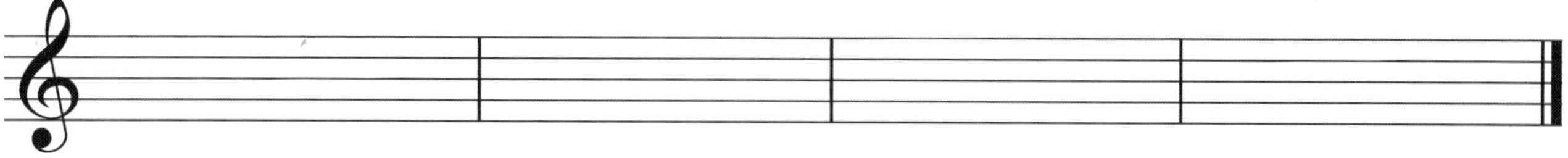

Check 1 Find out how much you remember.

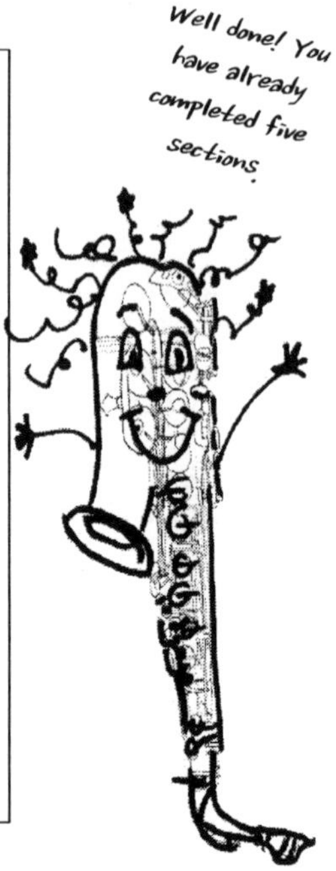
Well done! You have already completed five sections.

Mix and Match

Match the symbol to its name and number of beats.

Four quarter notes	Quarter rest
One quarter rest	Half note
Two quarter notes	Quarter note
One quarter note	Whole note

Quick Check

Are the letters correct. Tick or cross the answers.

G B C E G A F E D A B G C F A A

Quiz

True or false? Circle the right answer.

1. Music is divided into measures by bar lines. True False
2. Music is written on four lines called a staff. True False
3. Music uses the first eight letters of the alphabet. True False
4. Saxophone music is written mostly in bass clef. True False
5. A whole note is worth two half notes. True False
6. In music silence is shown by rests. True False

How many did you get right? 6

Time Signatures

$\frac{2}{4}$ 2 quarter note beats in a measure

$\frac{3}{4}$ 3 quarter note beats in a measure

$\frac{4}{4}$ or $\mathbf{C}$ 4 quarter note beats in a measure
$\mathbf{C}$ means Common Time

The top number shows how many beats are in a measure.

The bottom number shows what sort of beats. 4 represents quarter notes.

2 quarter note beats in a measure $\frac{2}{4}$

1   2   1   2   1   2   1   2

Copy the above rhythm.

3 quarter note beats in a measure $\frac{3}{4}$

1 2 3   1 2 3   1 2 3   1 2 3

Copy the above rhythm.

4 quarter note beats in a measure $\frac{4}{4}$

1 2 3 4   1 2 3 4   1 2 3 4   1 2 3 4   1 2 3 4

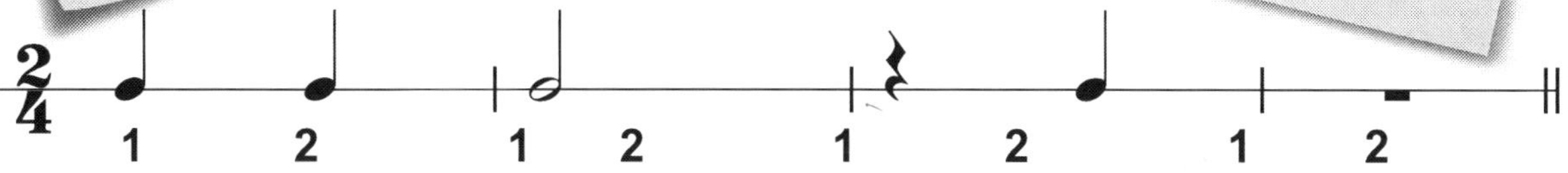

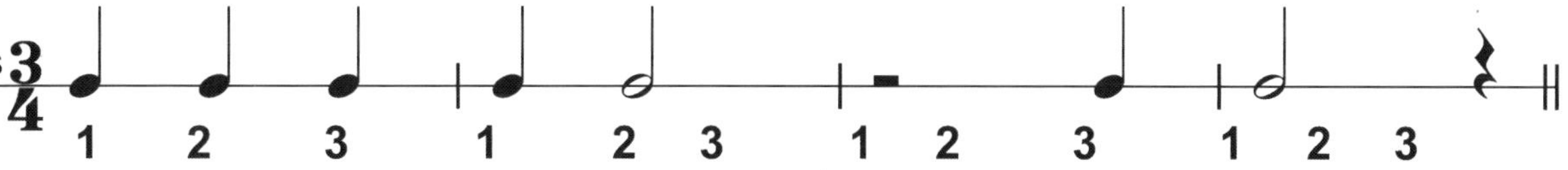

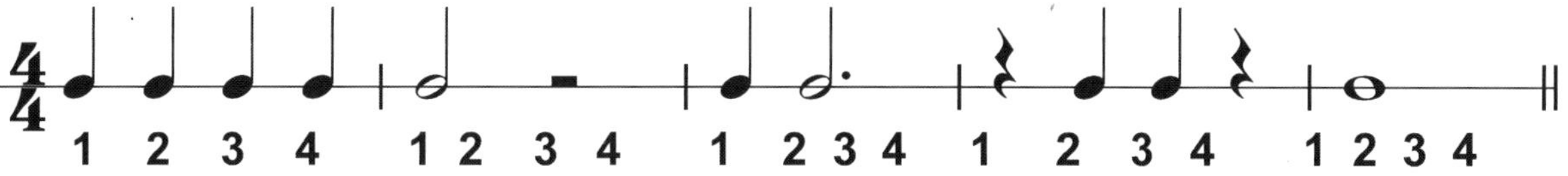

Copy the above rhythm.

Match the measure with its time signature.

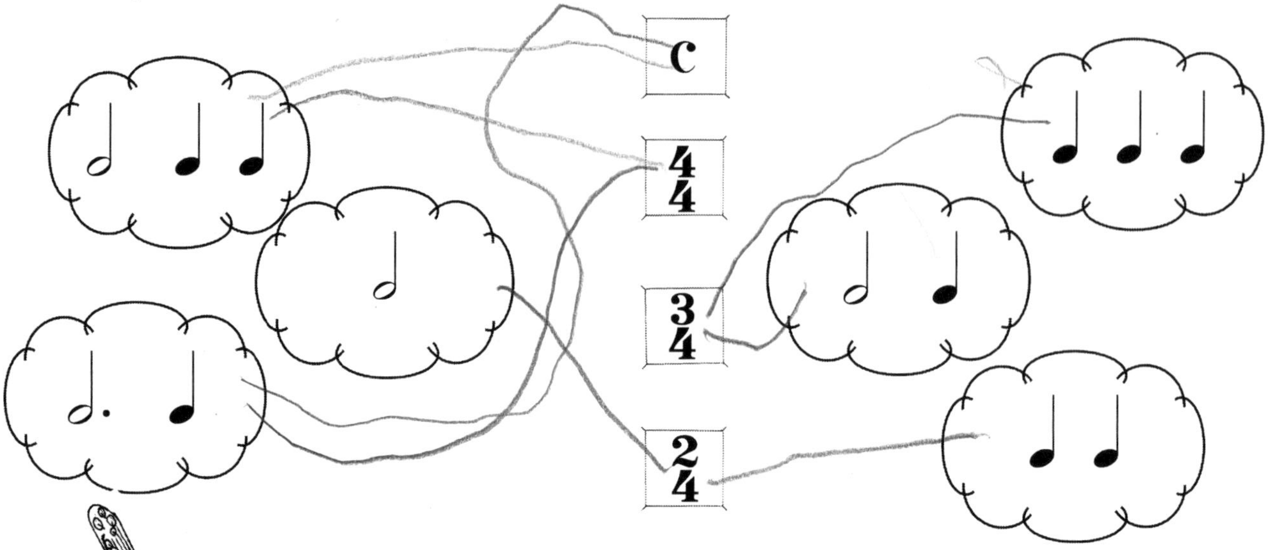

Count the beats in a measure and write in the time signatures.

Write in the counts.

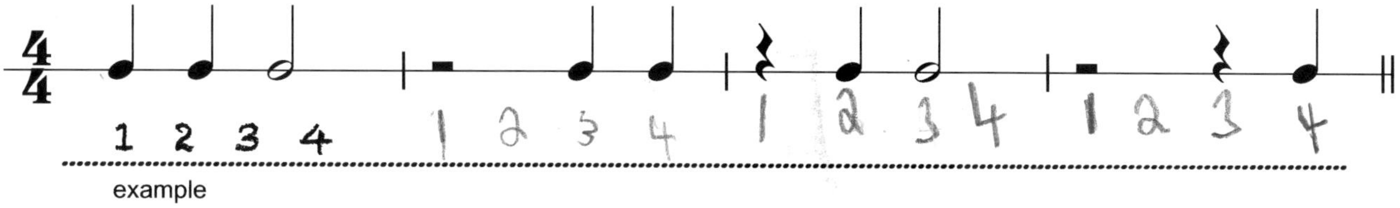

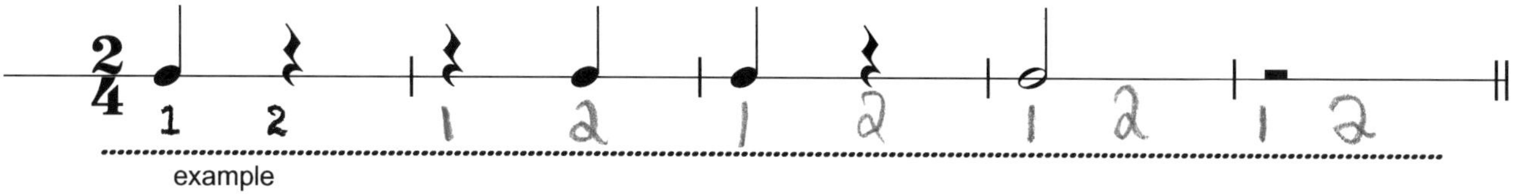

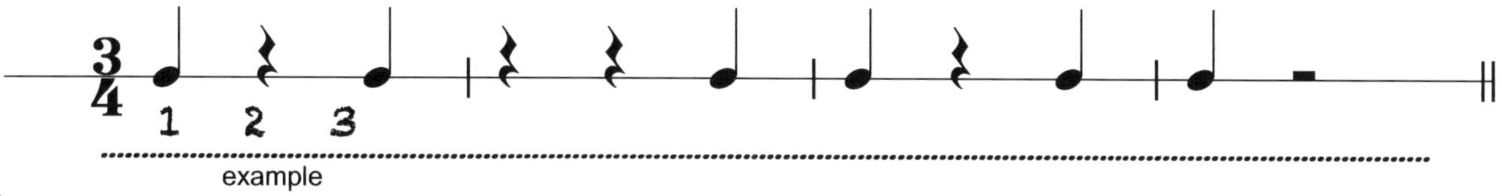

*Count the beats in a measure and add the missing notes at the *.*

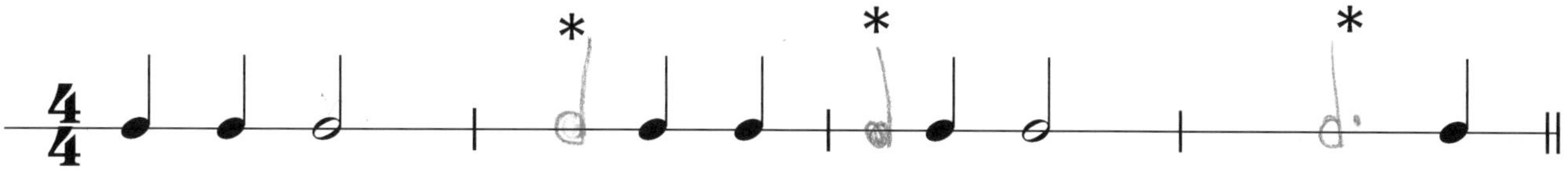

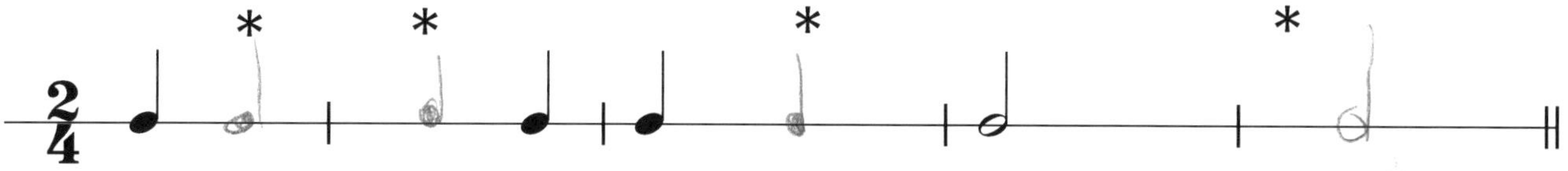

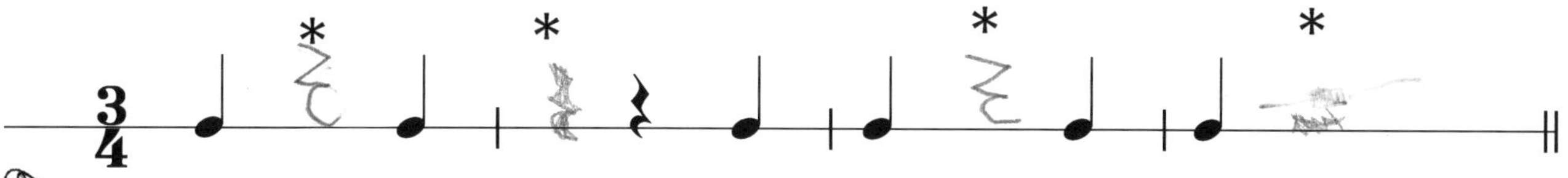

Fill each measure with notes of different lengths to fit with time signature.

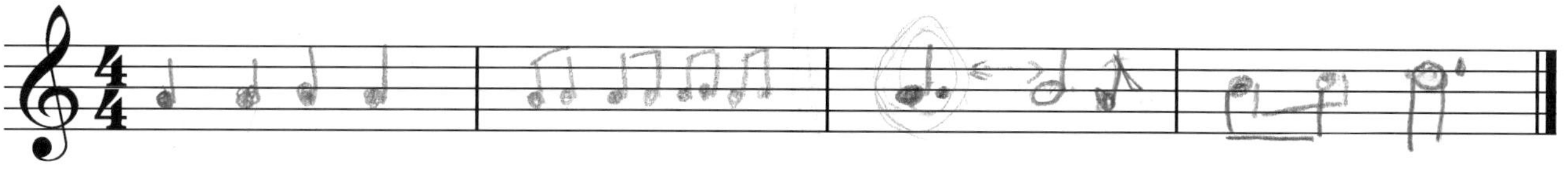

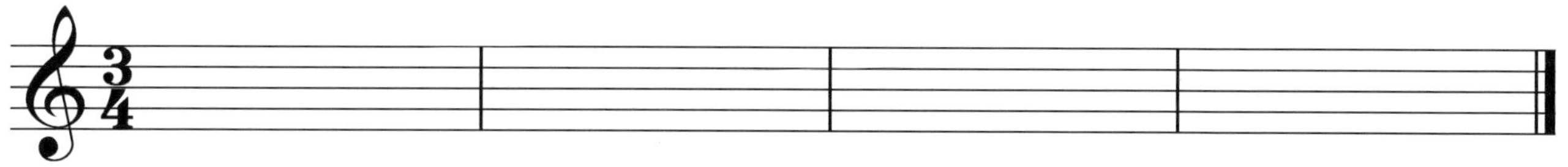

Accidentals

An accidental is a sharp, flat or natural that occurs in a piece of music.

♯ **Sharp** — *A sharp raises a note.*

♭ **Flat** — *A flat lowers a note.*

♮ **Natural** — *A natural restores a note to its original pitch.*

An accidental is written in front of a note.

An accidental changes every following note in the measure that is on the same space or line.

An accidental is written on the same line or in the same space as the note.

Write a sharp before each note.

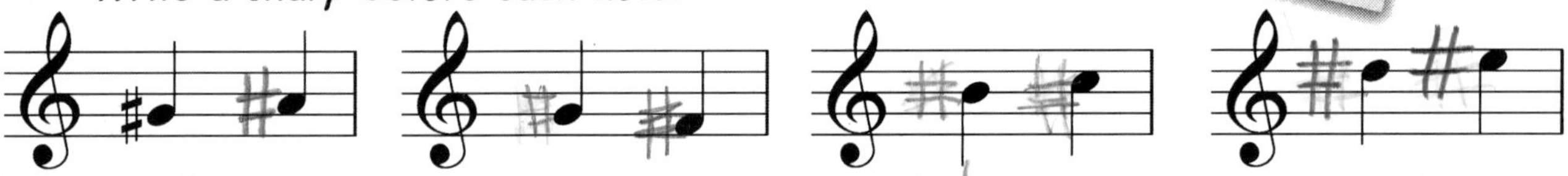

example

Write a flat before each note.

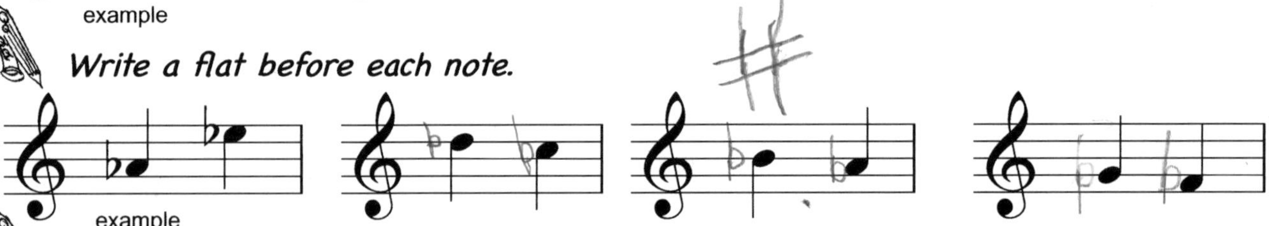

example

Write a natural before each note.

example

Name the notes.

....

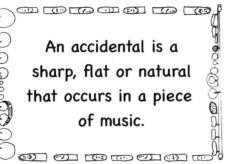

....

Name the notes.

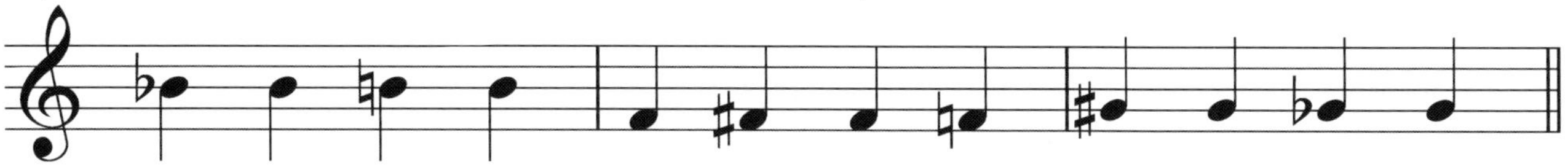

....

Write the notes.

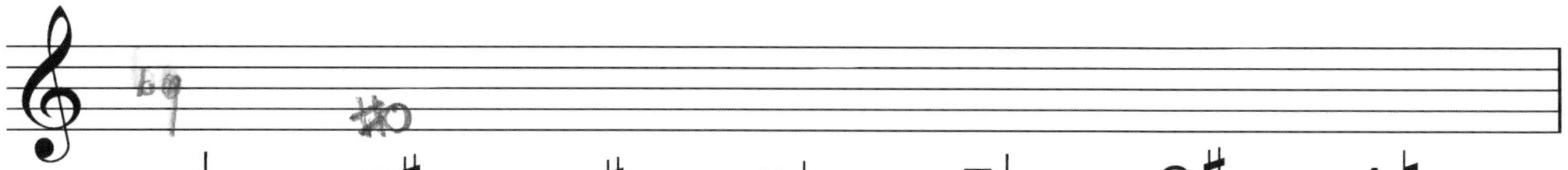

B♭ F♯ G♯ B♮ E♭ C♯ A♮

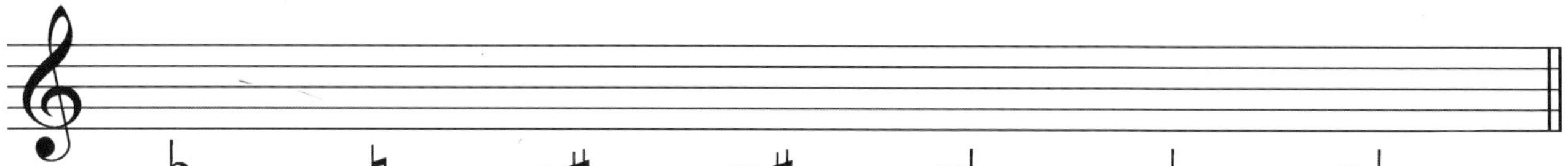

G♭ D♮ A♯ E♯ F♭ D♭ C♭

Write notes with accidentals but of different lengths so that every measure fits with the time signature.

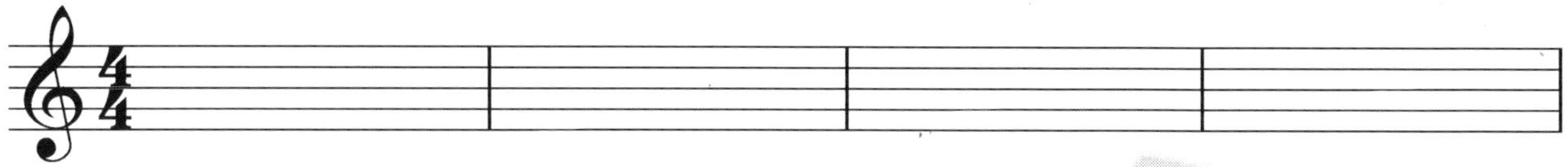

When notes have the same letter name but are different pitches, another accidental is written.

Name the notes.

G♯ G♯
example

....

Write a tune in which every note is a flat.

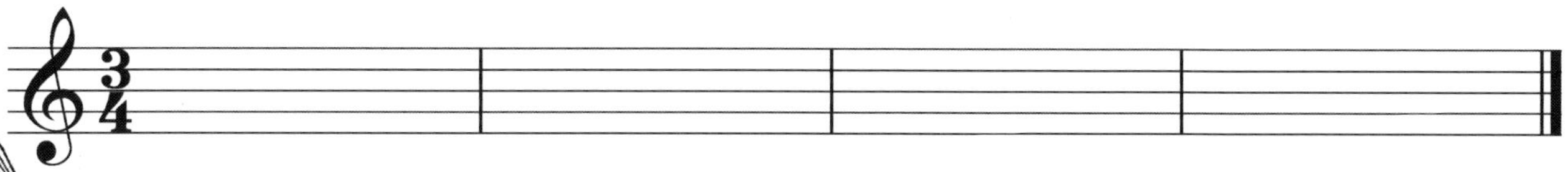

Write a tune in which every note is a sharp.

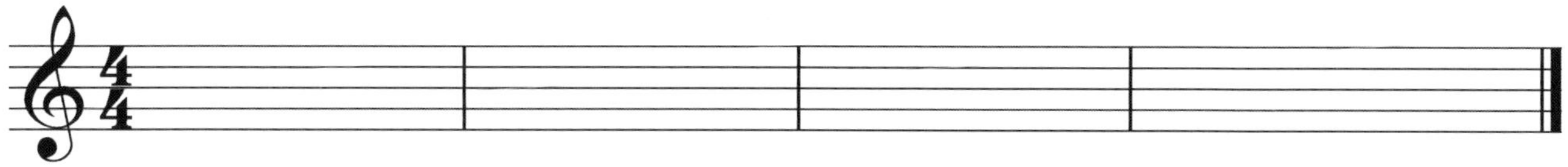

Eighth Notes

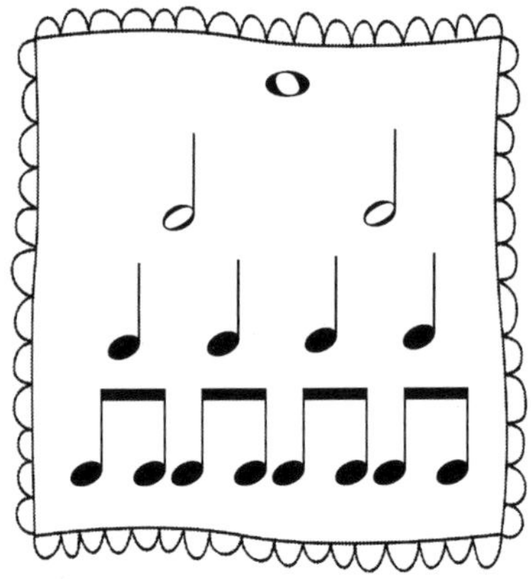

Eighth notes

Eighth rest

A eighth note is half of one quarter note.

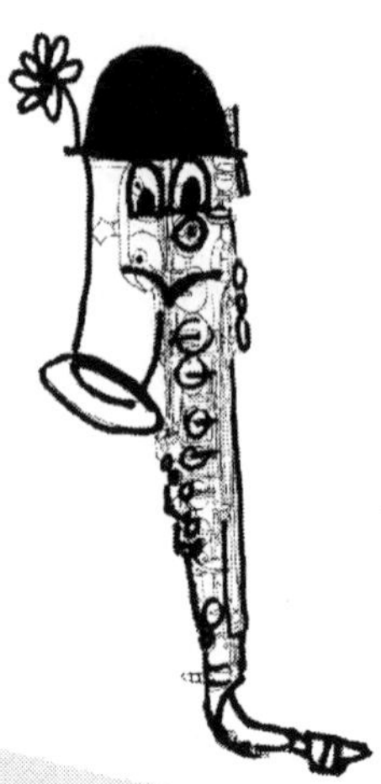

Two eighth notes are usually beamed together to form a quarter note beat.

The flag is always drawn on the right side of the stem.

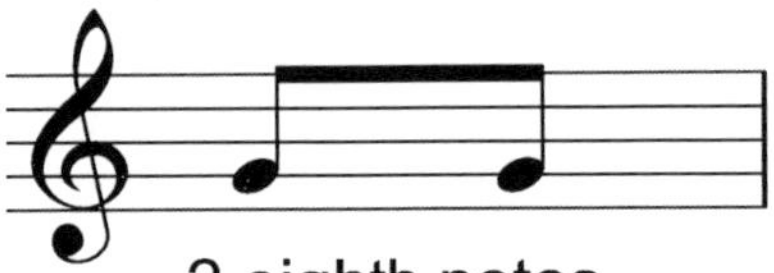

2 eighth notes

=

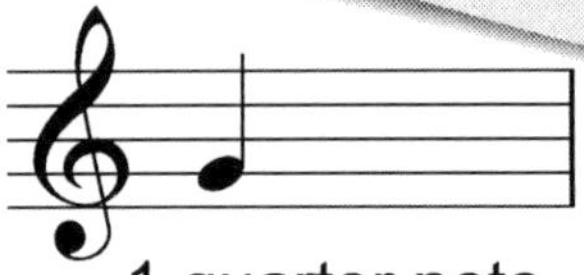

1 quarter note

4 eighth notes

=

1 half note

The first and/or last four eighth notes in a measure can be beamed together if they form half the bar, but never the middle four.

8 eighth notes

=

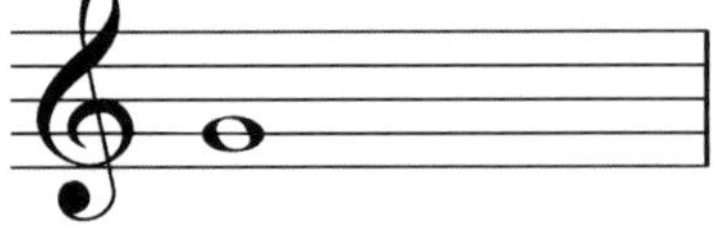

1 whole note

Write groups of eighth notes and quarter notes, Remember to check how many quarter note beats are in a measure.

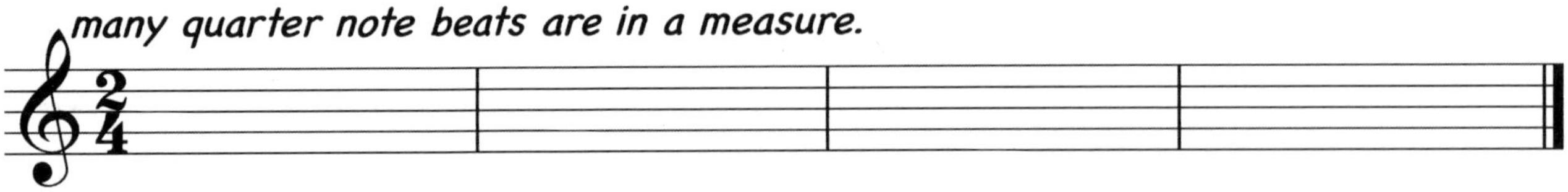

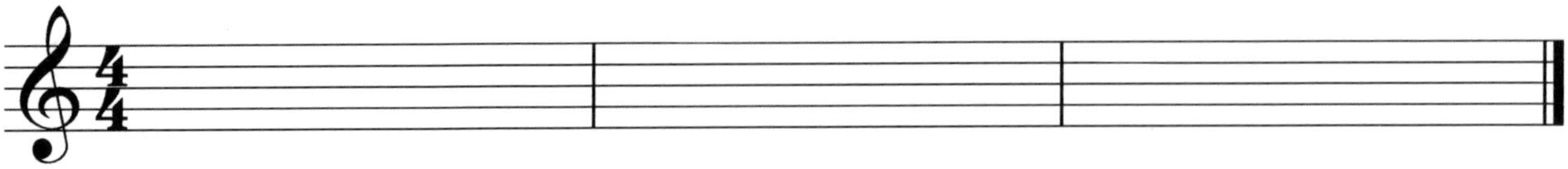

Fill in the numbers.

1 whole note = ☐ half note

1 half note = ☐ quarter notes

1 quarter note = ☐ eighth notes

Join the shapes that have the same number of beats.

Finish writing in the counts.

1 + 2 + 3 + 4 + 1 2 + 3 + 4

1 2 + 3 4

1 2 3 4

Write notes of different lengths to fit with the time signature. Use any notes.

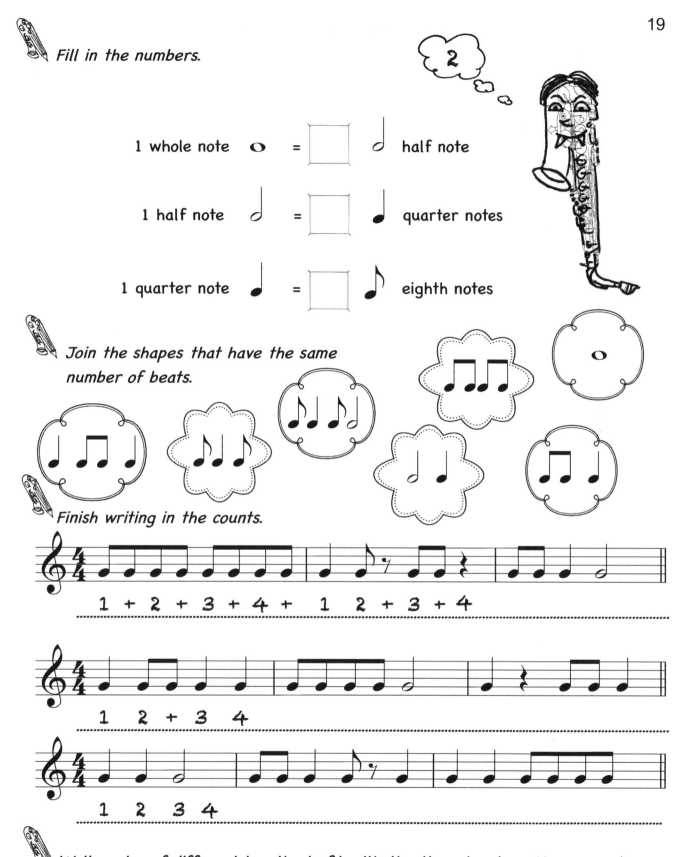

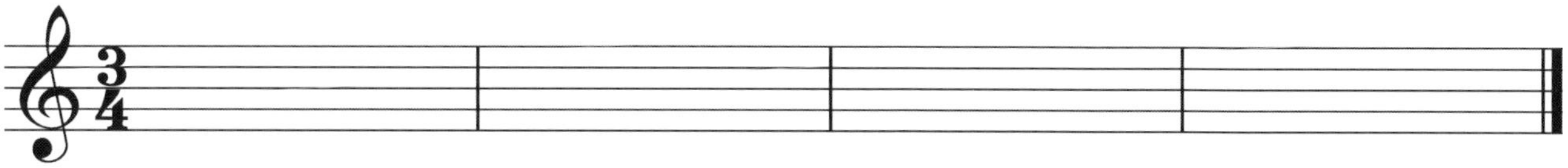

Ledger Lines

Ledger lines extend the staff up and down. Notes are written in exactly the right position.

Ledger (or leger) lines are small lines for notes written above or below the staff.

Ledger lines are like an invisible staff.

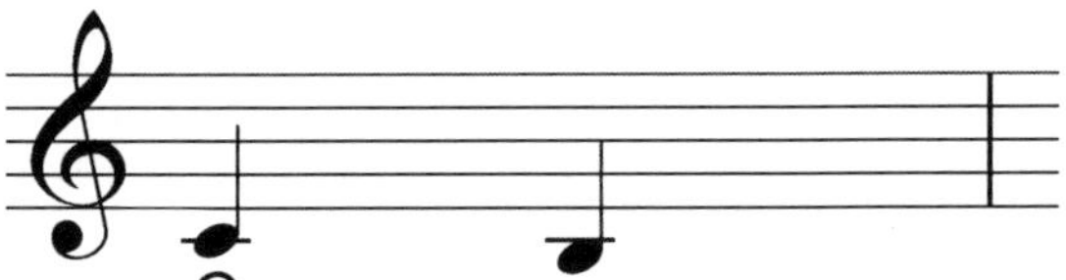

C B

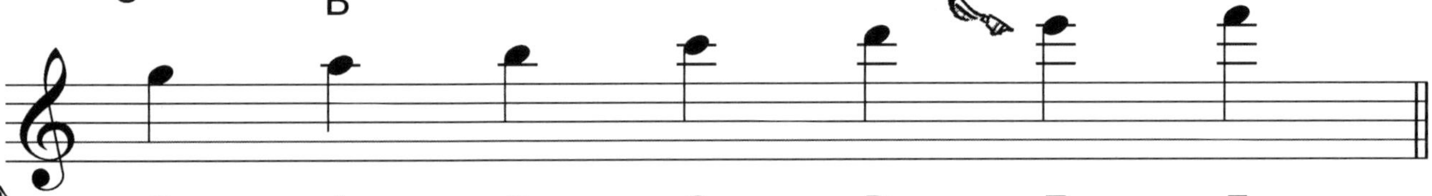

G A B C D E F

Name these notes.

....

Join the notes to the correct letter name.

D **C** **B** **G** **B** **C** **A** **D**

Write these notes using high and low ledger lines.

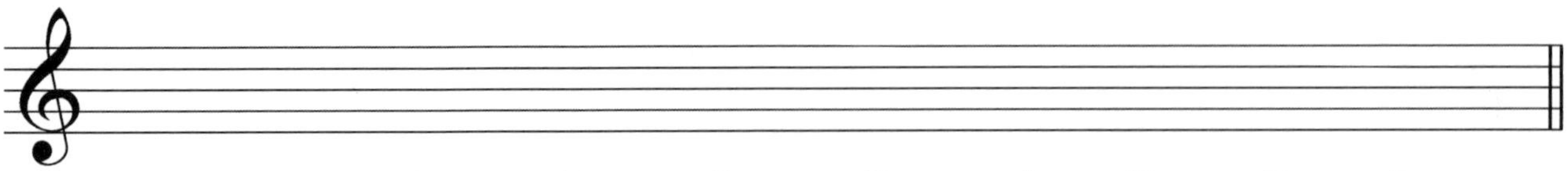

D A C B C D A E D G

Check 2 How much do you remember?

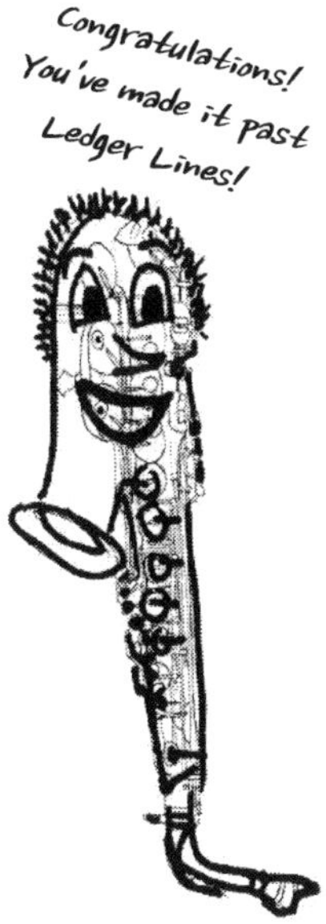
Congratulations!
You've made it past
Ledger Lines!

Mix and Match

Match the time signature to its description.

Four quarter notes in a measure	$\frac{2}{4}$
Three quarter notes in a measure	$\frac{4}{4}$
Two quarter notes in a measure	$\frac{3}{4}$

Quick Check

Are the letter names correct? Tick or cross the answers.

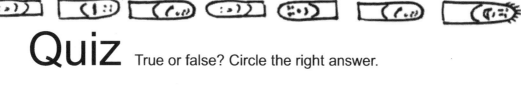

G B♭ C♯ F C A D A♭ D A E♭ D C F♭ E♭ A♯

Quiz

True or false? Circle the right answer.

1. Two eighth notes add up to one quarter note. True False
2. Four eighth notes add up to one half note. True False
3. A natural sign is not an accidental. True False
4. A time signature's top number tells us what sort of beat is in a measure. True False
5. A time signature's bottom number tells us what sort of beat is in a measure. True False

How many did you get right? ☐

Major Scales

All major scales have the same tune based on the steps between notes.

The steps that make up a scale are called whole steps and half steps.

Scales are a series of notes going up and down in steps.

An octave is an interval of eight notes. From low C to high C is an octave.

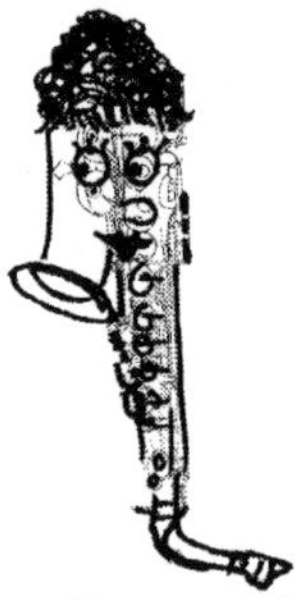

All major scales have the same pattern of whole steps and half steps.

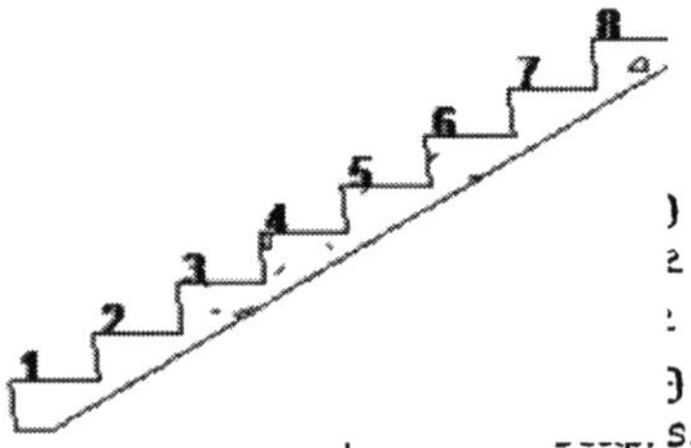

C major scale (one octave) ascending and descending

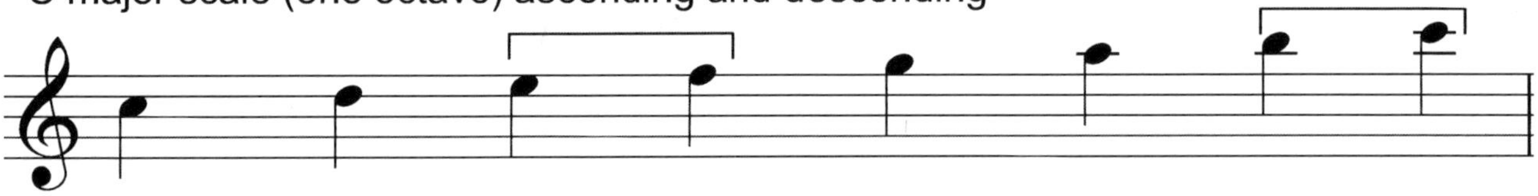

whole step whole step half step whole step whole step whole step half step

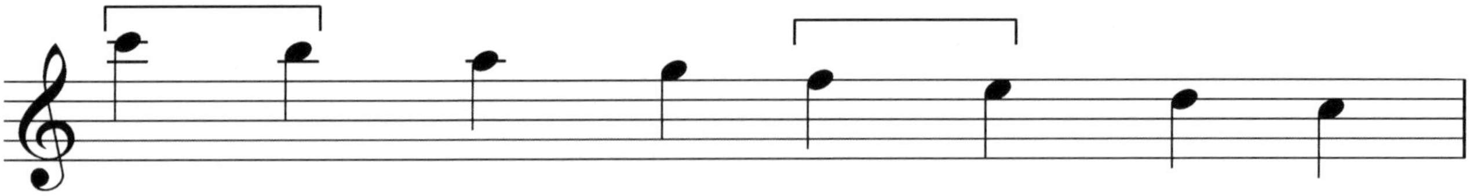

half step whole step whole step whole stephalf step whole step whole step

Draw a bracket above the half step intervals.

G major scale (one octave) ascending

F major scale (one octave) ascending

Write the missing notes and name the scale.

C ....

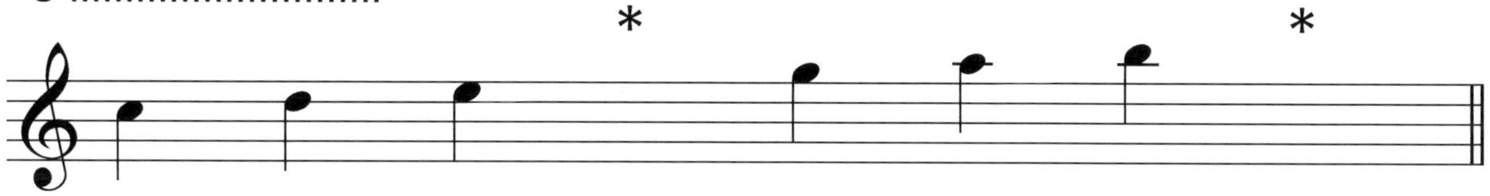

....

....

....

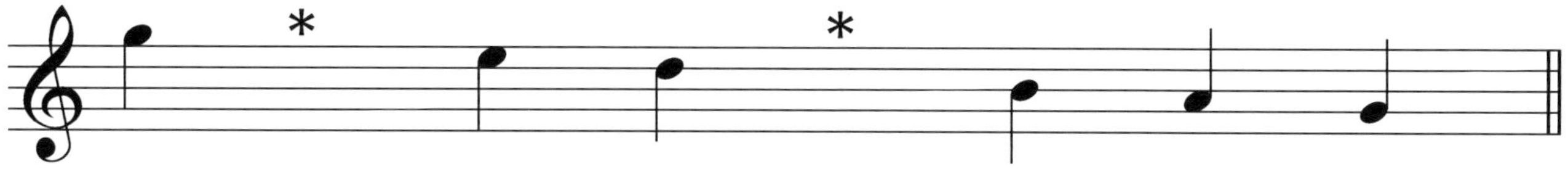

....

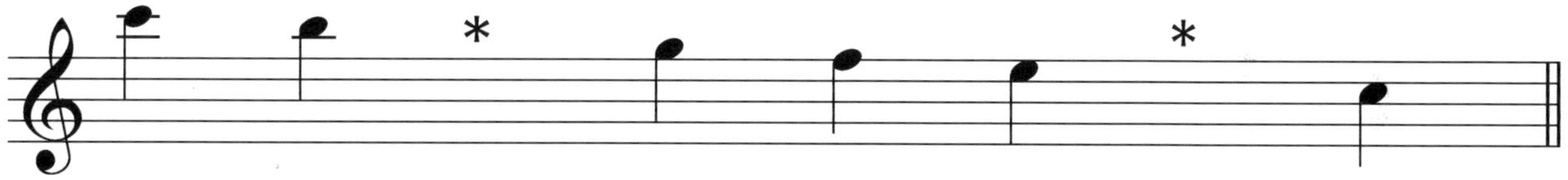

....

Copy the scale exactly.

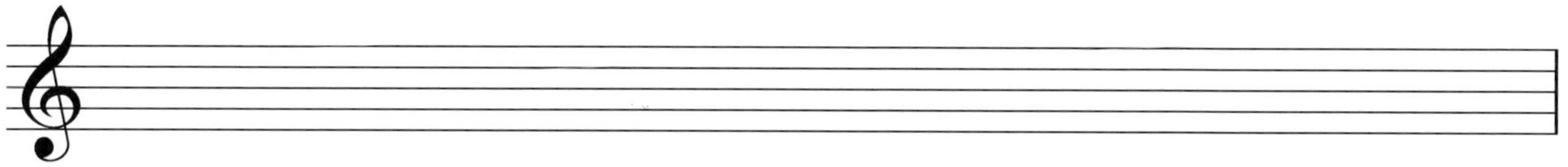

Key Signatures

Key signatures are sharps or flats at the start of each staff and show which scale is being used in the music.

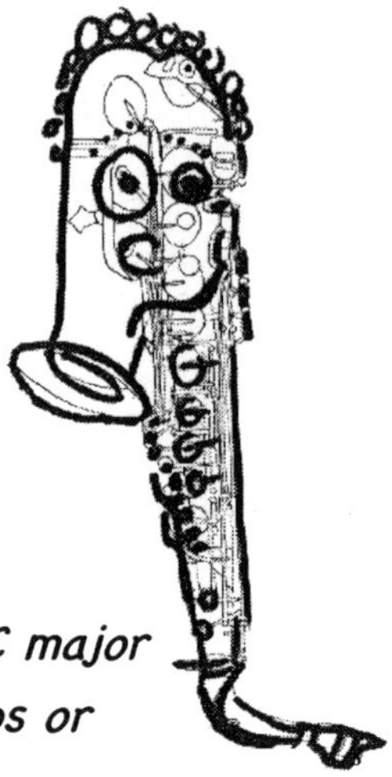

The key signature of one sharp is always F♯.

The key signature of one flat is always B♭.

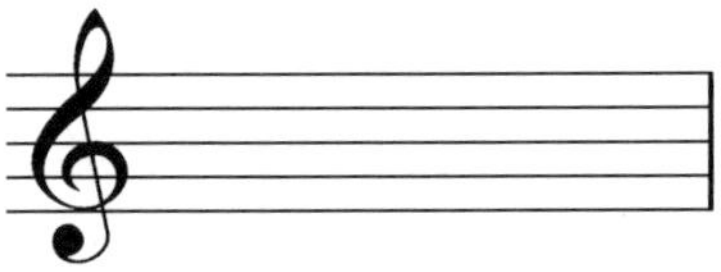

The key of C major has no sharps or flats.

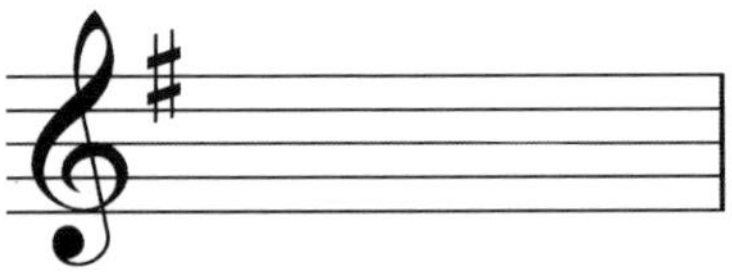

The key of G major has one sharp, F♯.

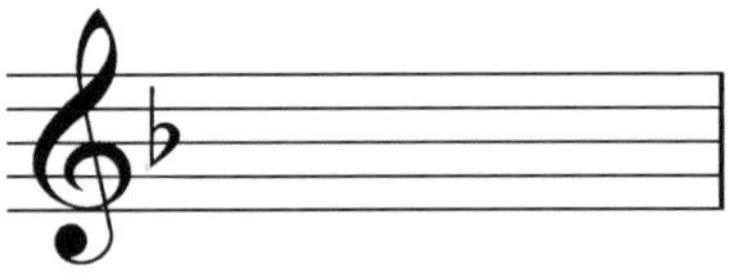

The key of F major has one flat, B♭.

Join the key name to the key signature.

G major

F major

C major

No sharps or flats

F♯

B♭

Write the key signatures.

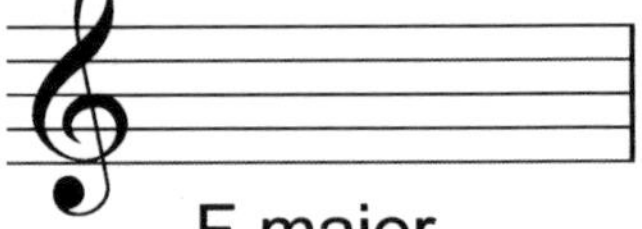

F major

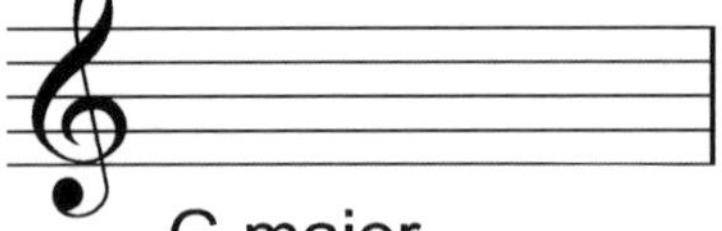

G major

In what key is this phrase? ....

In what key is this phrase? ....

Write the treble clef and the key signature for these scales.

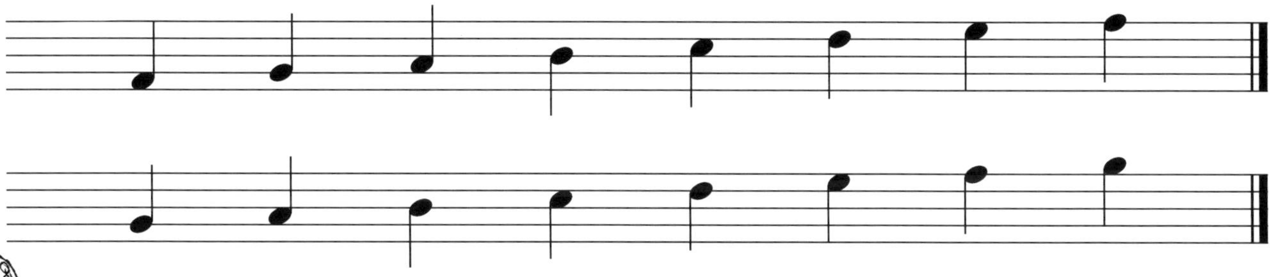

Write the treble clef, the key signature and the scale of F major ascending.

Write the treble clef, the key signature and the scale of G major ascending.

Sometimes the key of a tune or phrase is shown by accidentals, perhaps because it has changed key.

Is there an accidental?

Write the key of this phrase

....

Write the key of this phrase.

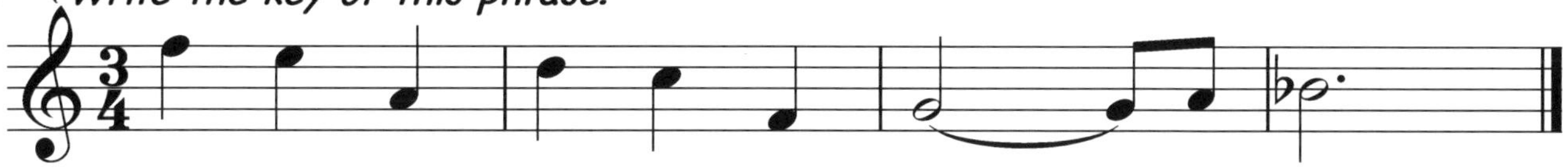

....

But where are the flats and sharps?

Write the key of this phrase.

....

Write a phrase in F major that includes accidentals. Start and finish on F.

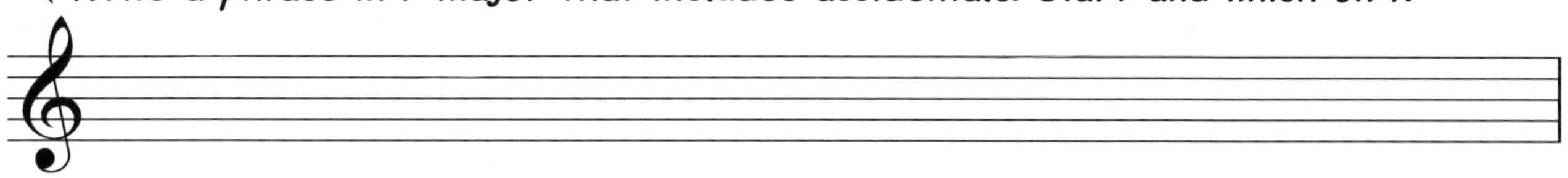

Dotted Quarter Notes

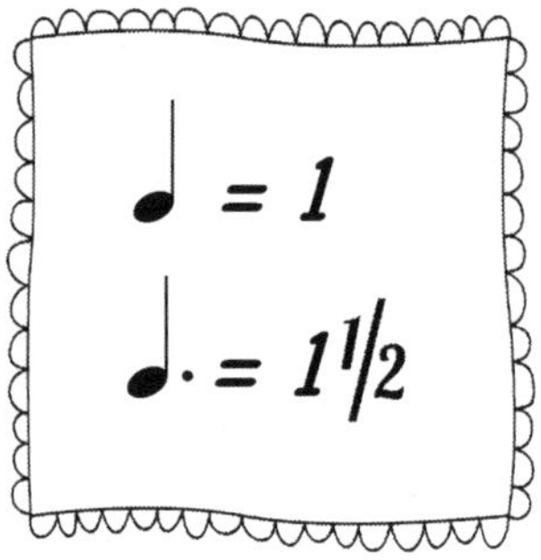

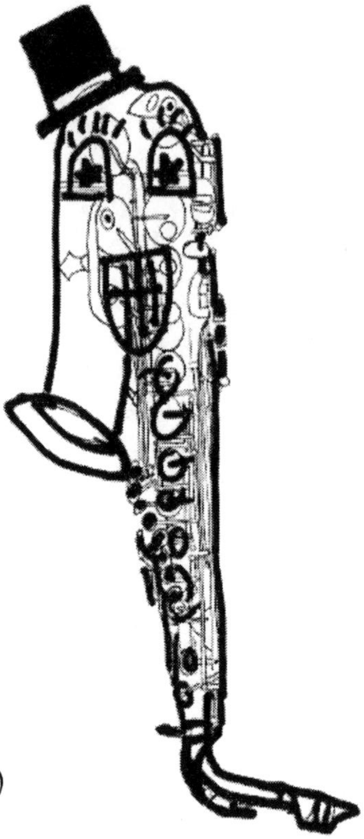

♩· Dotted quarter note
𝄾· Dotted quarter rest

A dot after a note adds
half its value to that note.

♩· $= 1\frac{1}{2}$

♩· = ♩ + ♪
$1\frac{1}{2} = 1 + \frac{1}{2}$

♩· = ♪ + ♪ + ♪
$1\frac{1}{2} = \frac{1}{2} + \frac{1}{2} + \frac{1}{2}$

1 2 + 3 4

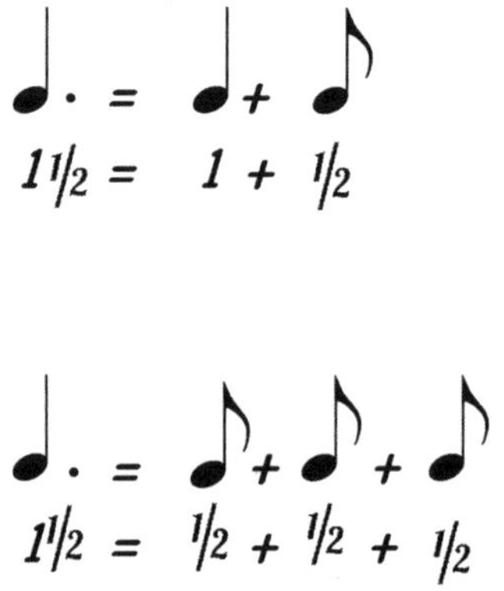

A dotted quarter note is
often followed by an eighth
note. Together they add up
to 2 quarter notes.

Add up the notes and match them to the counts.

  $\boxed{2}$ $\boxed{1\frac{1}{2}}$ $\boxed{4}$

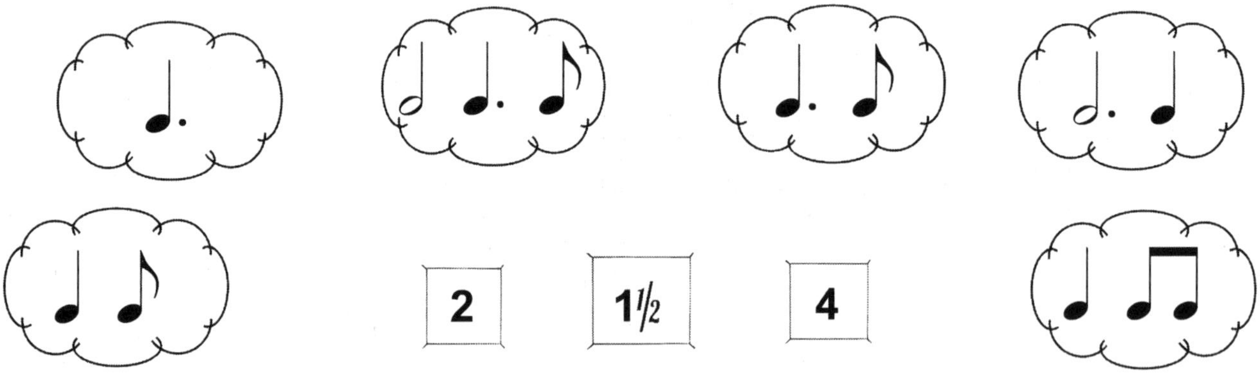

 Write a dotted quarter note rhythm in each measure.

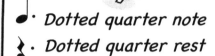

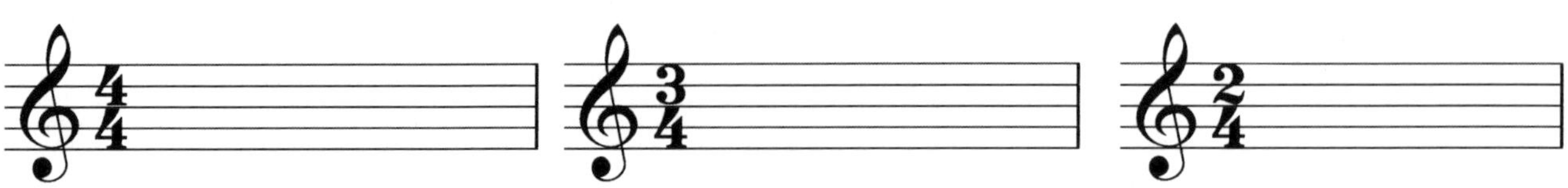

Write the number of beats in the box.

𝅝 = ☐ *quarter notes*

𝅝. = ☐ *half notes*

𝅗𝅥 = ☐ *eighth notes*

𝅘𝅥 = ☐ *eighth notes*

𝅝. = ☐ *quarter notes*

𝅗𝅥. = ☐ *quarter notes*

𝅘𝅥. = ☐ *quarter notes*

𝅗𝅥. = ☐ *eighth notes*

𝅘𝅥. = ☐ *eighth notes*

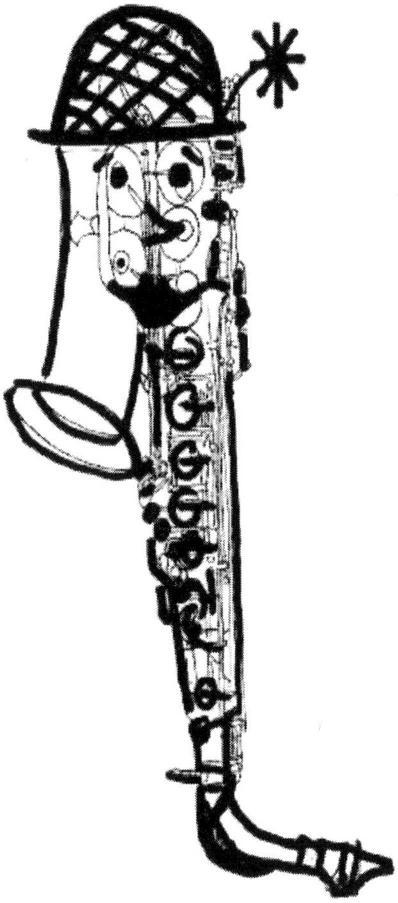

Write in the missing quarter note counts.

1 2+ … … … … 34 1 + … … … … + 1 … … …

Copy the above tune exactly.

Write a phrase that includes a dotted quarter note rhythm. Begin and end on G.

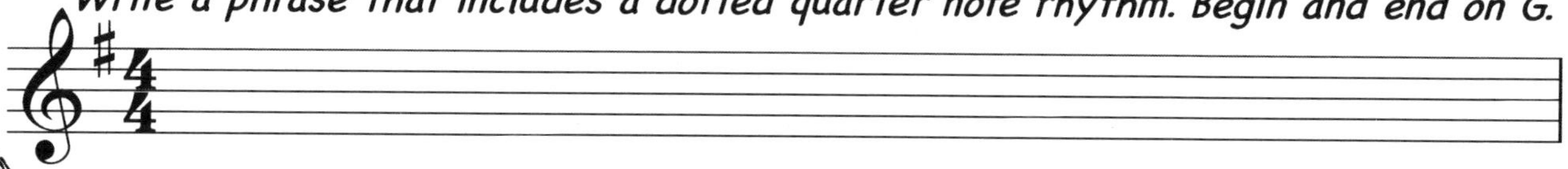

Write a phrase that includes a dotted quarter note rhythm. Begin and end on C.

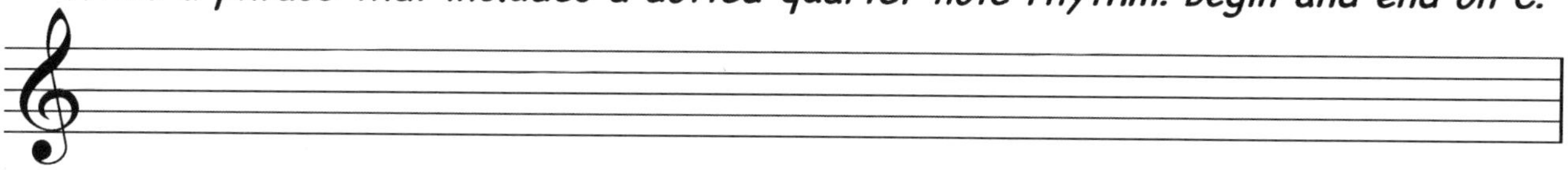

Add a dotted note to make each measure the correct length.

Match the note with the rest of the same length.

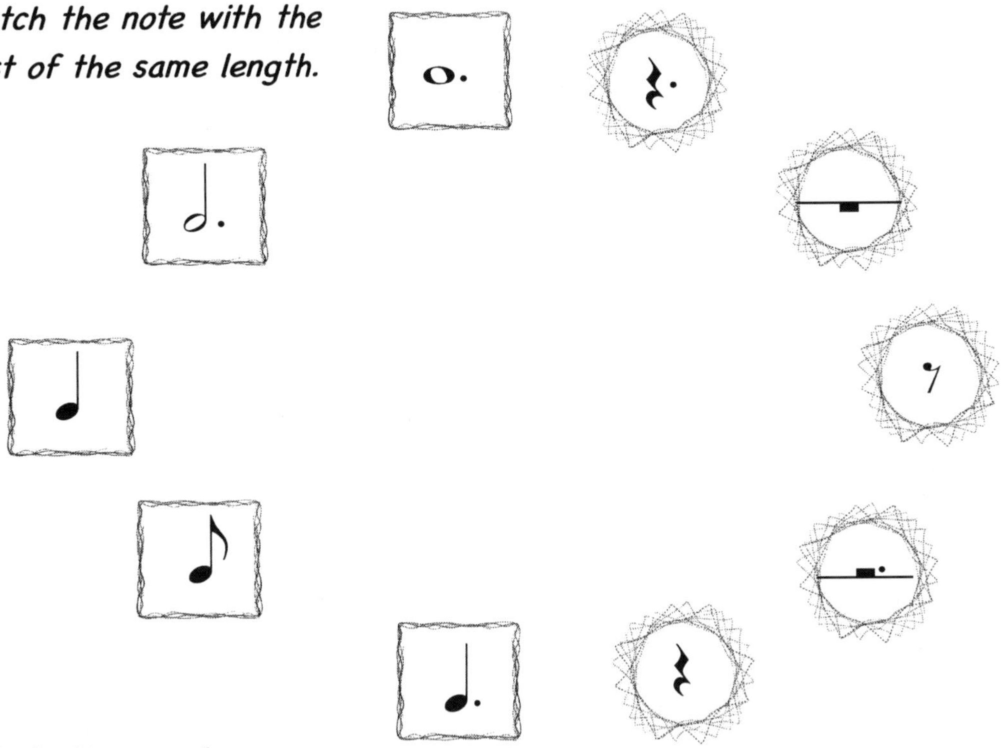

Write in the counts.

Write the scale of G major in dotted quarter notes and eigth notes.

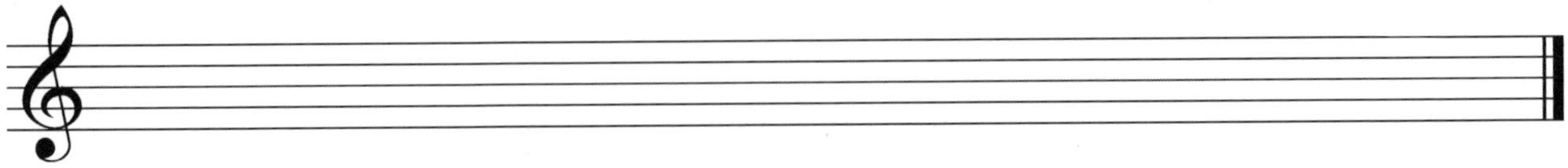

Write the scale of F major in dotted quarter notes and eighth notes.

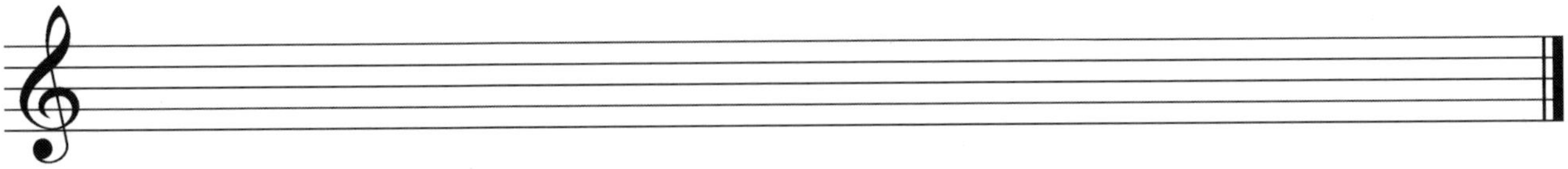

Check 3 How much do you remember?

Hurray! You are more than half way through the book. Good going!

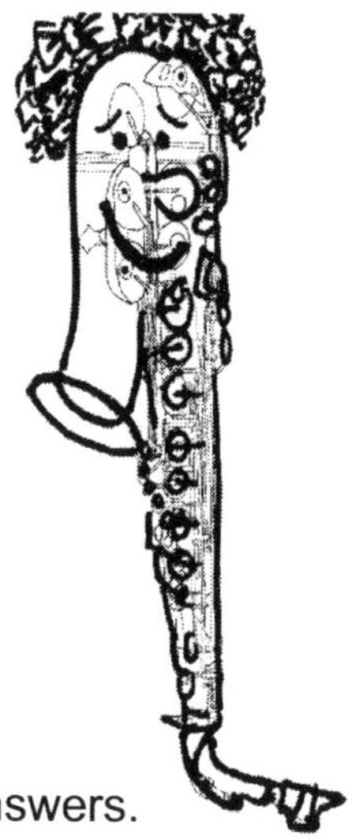

Mix and Match
Match the scale with its key signature.

C major scale	F♯
G major scale	B♭
F major scale	No ♯ No ♭

Quick Check
Are the key signatures correct? Tick or cross the answers.

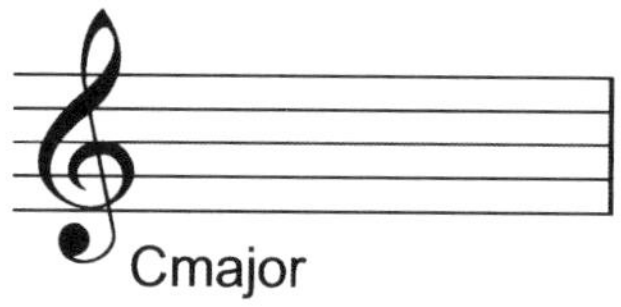

Cmajor

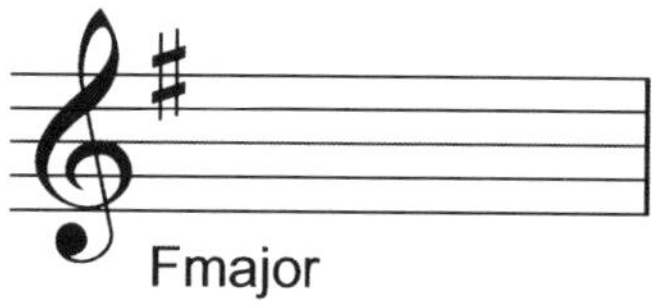

Fmajor

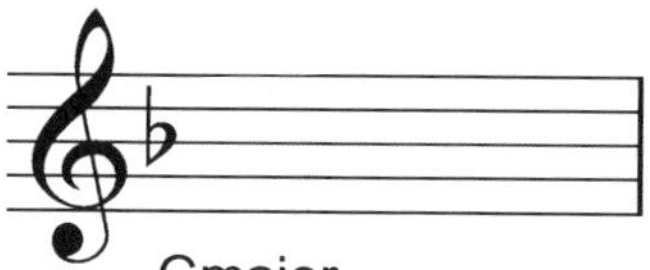

Gmajor

Quiz
True or false? Circle the right answer.

1. A dot next to a note doubles the note in length. **True** **False**

2. Key signatures are written at the start of a line. **True** **False**

3. The scale of G major has B flat. **True** **False**

4. Half steps and whole steps are intervals between notes. **True** **False**

5. All major scales have different patterns of whole steps and half steps. **True** **False**

How many did you get right? ☐

Degrees of the Scale

Degrees of the Scale

The first note of a scale is the keynote or 1st degree. The second note is the 2nd degree and the third is the 3rd degree. This contunues until the 8th degree or octave.

Degrees of the Scale

C major

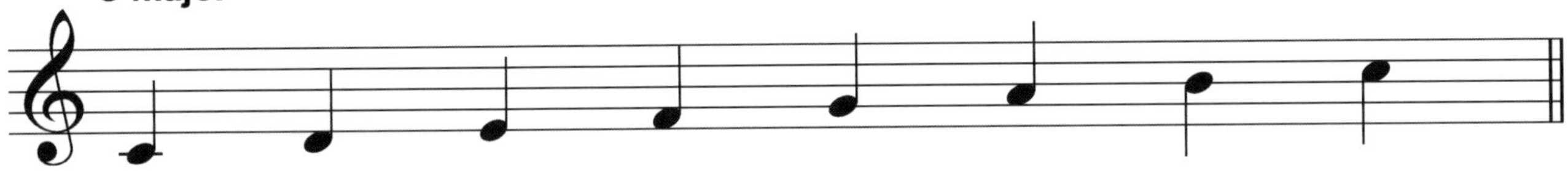

Write the degree of the scale in the key of C major.

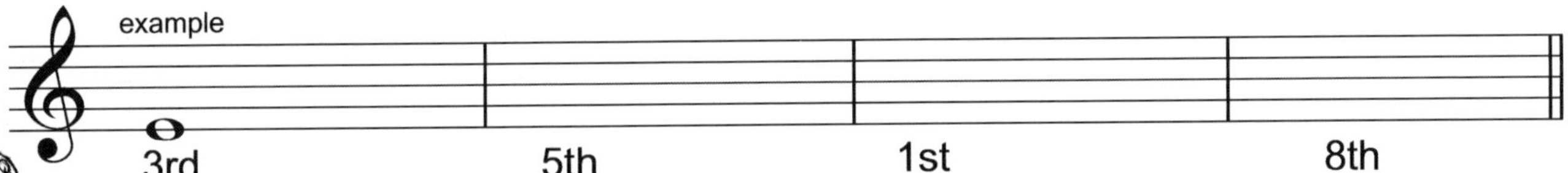

Write the degree of the scale in the key of F major. (F is the 1st degree)

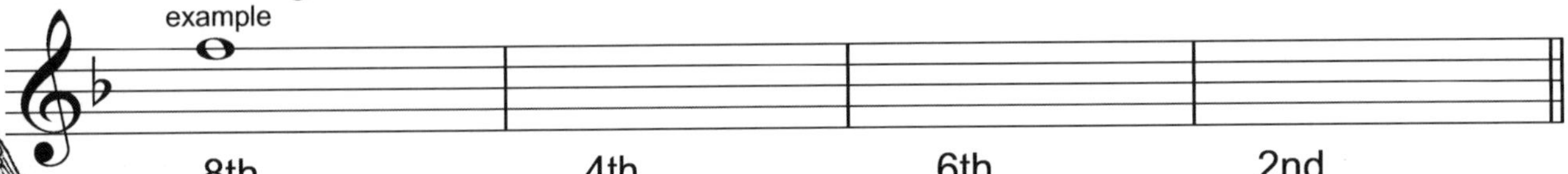

Write the degree of the scale in the key of G major. (G is the 1st degree)

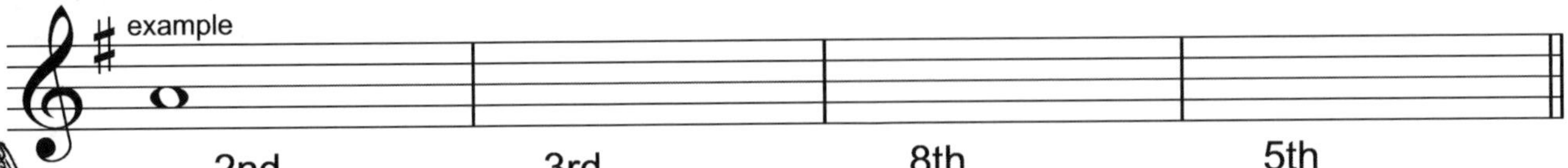

Write a phrase in C major using only the 1st, 2nd, 3rd and 5th degrees of the scale.

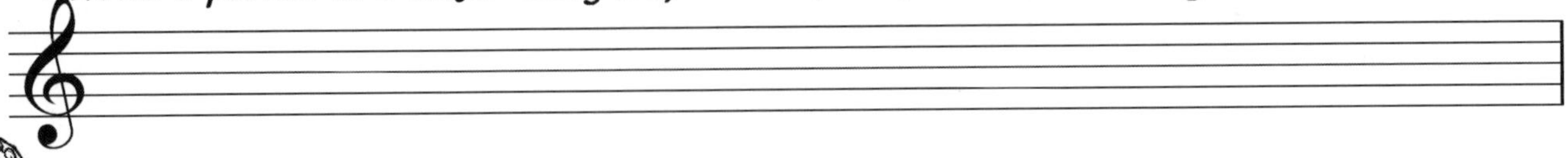

Write a phrase in G major using only the 8th, 6th, 5th and 4th degrees of the scale.

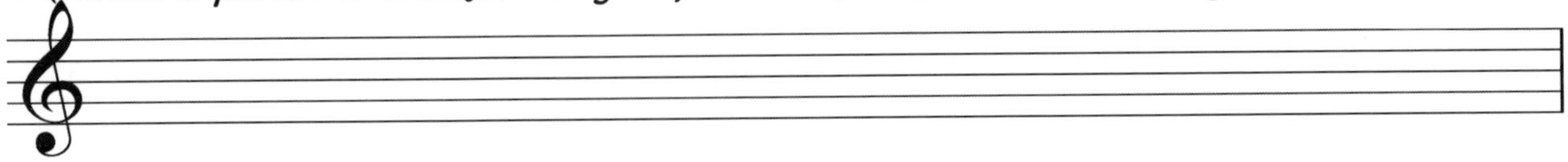

Intervals

An interval is the distance between two notes.

C major

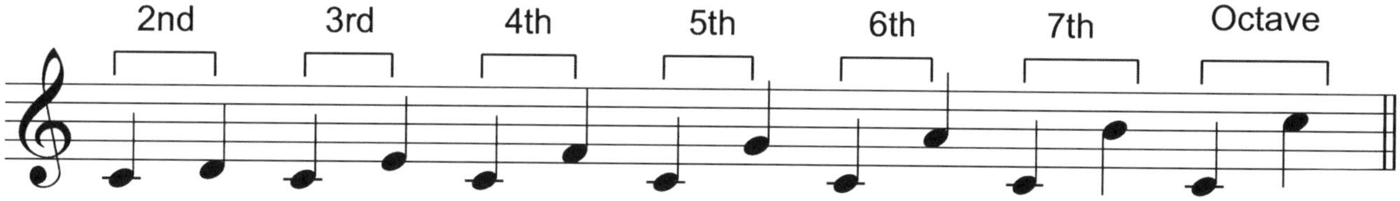

F major

Write in the interval numbers.

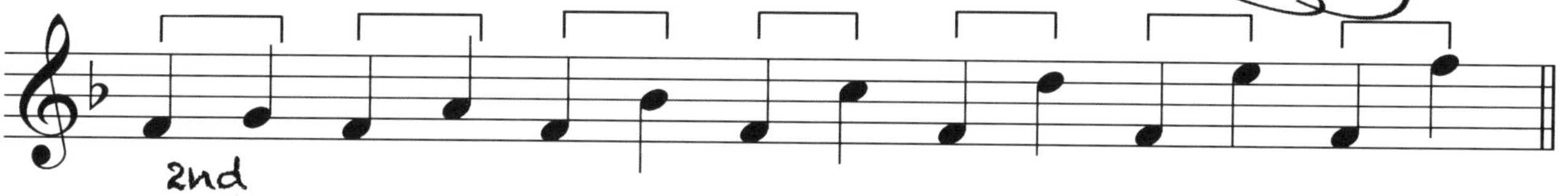

2nd
example

Write the missing notes for the intervals in G major.

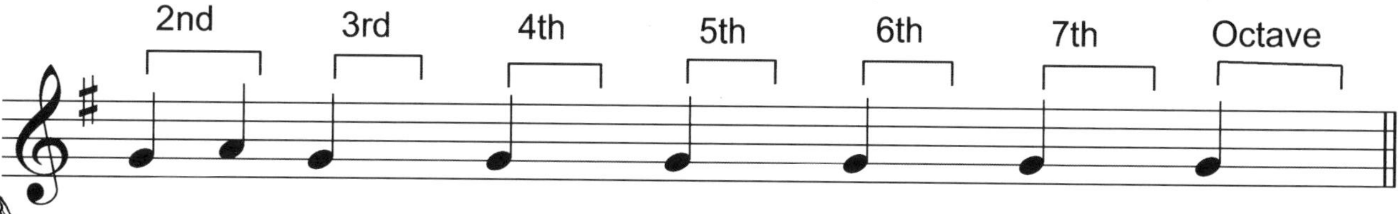

Write the intervals.

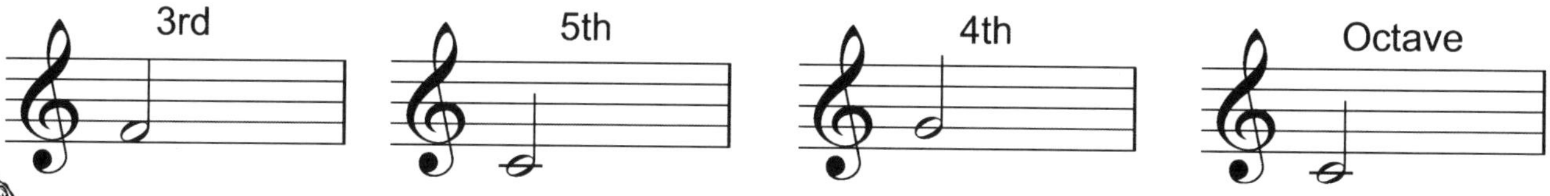

Using any note as the lowest note, write a phrase with only 3rds and 5ths.

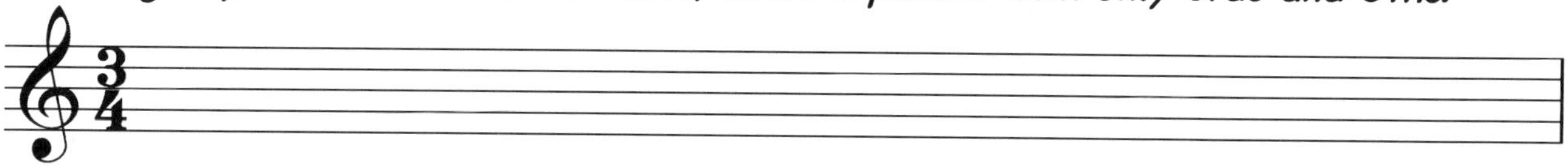

Match the interval with its description.

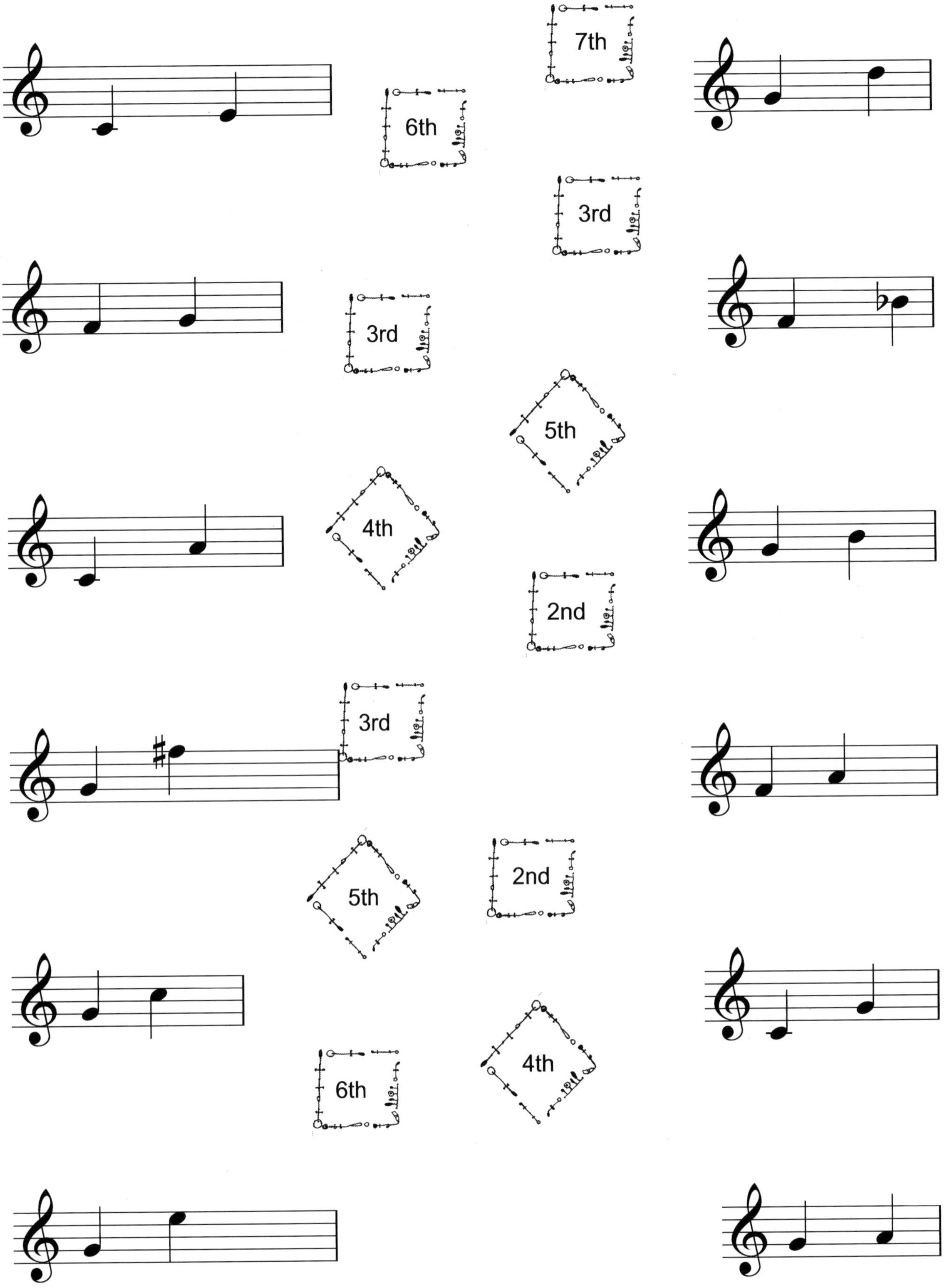

Minor Scales

Relatives
Each minor scale shares a key signature with a major scale. They are related.

The relative minor keynote is the sixth note of the major scale.

There are three kinds of minor scale. They are:
the natural minor scale,
the harmonic minor scale,
the melodic minor scale.
(In Book 2)

The natural minor scale has exactly the same notes as its relative major. But it starts on the 6th note of the major scale.

In C major, the sixth note of the scale is A. So A minor is the relative minor.

A natural minor scale (relative major is C major)

whole step half step whole step whole step half step whole step whole step

Draw a bracket above the half step intervals.

D natural minor scale (relative major is F major)

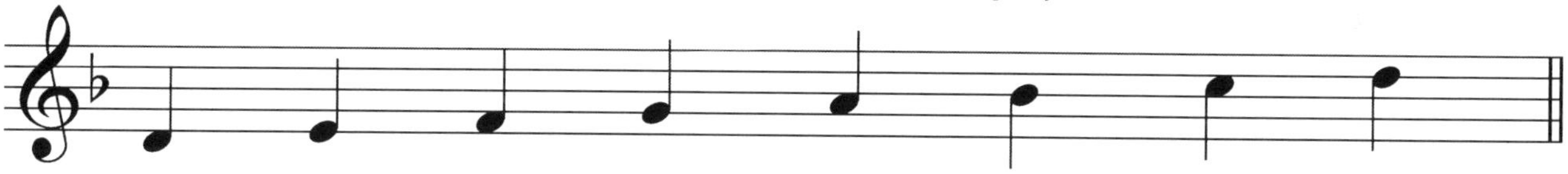

whole step half step whole step whole step half step whole step whole step

Draw a bracket above the half step intervals.

E natural minor scale (relative major is G major)

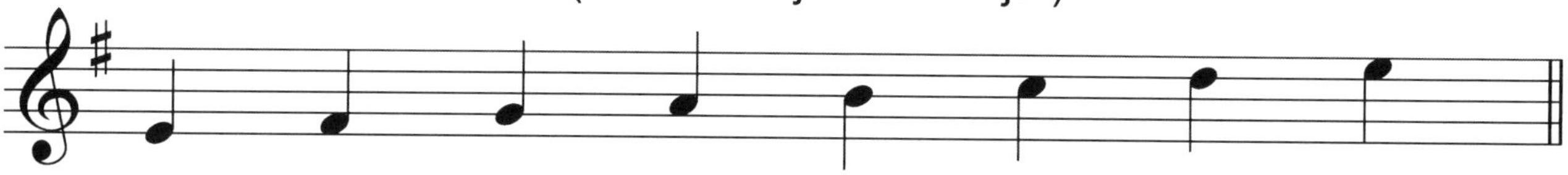

Write a phrase using only the notes of the A natural minor scale. Begin and end on A.

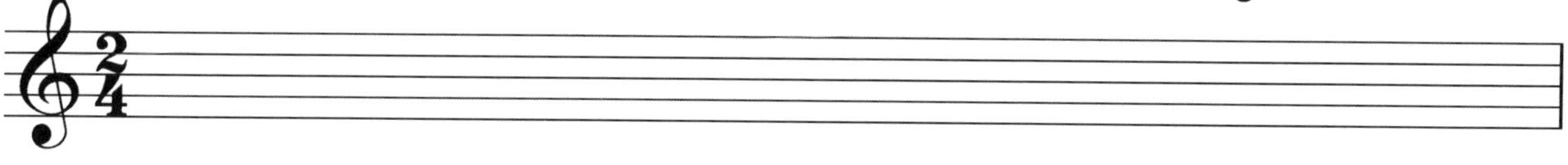

Write in the missing notes and name the scale.

A ....

....

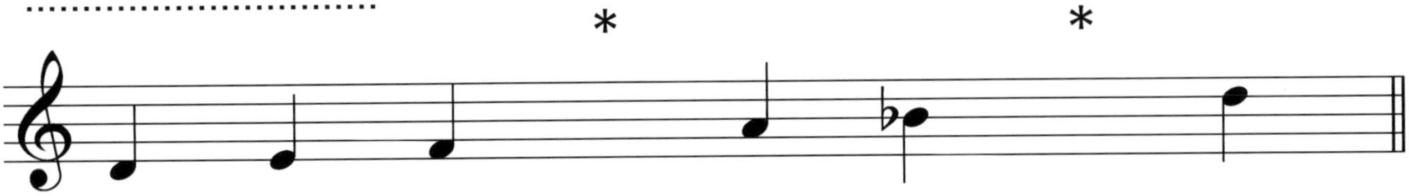

....

....

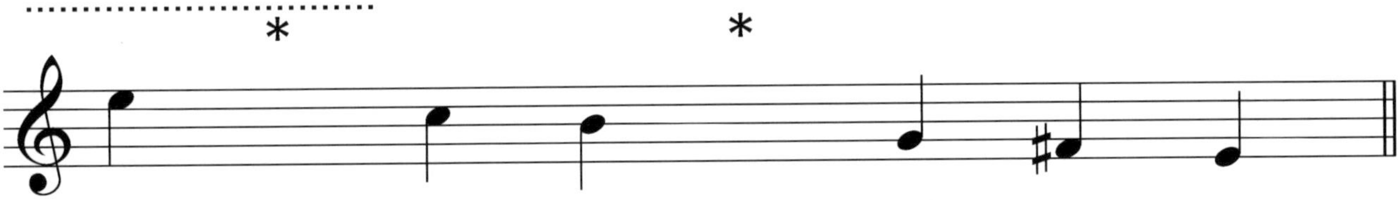

....

....

Write in the A natural minor scale ascending and descending.

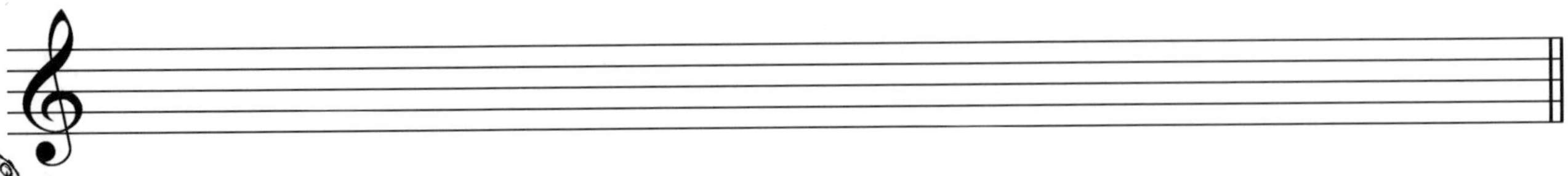

Write in the E natural minor scale ascending and descending.

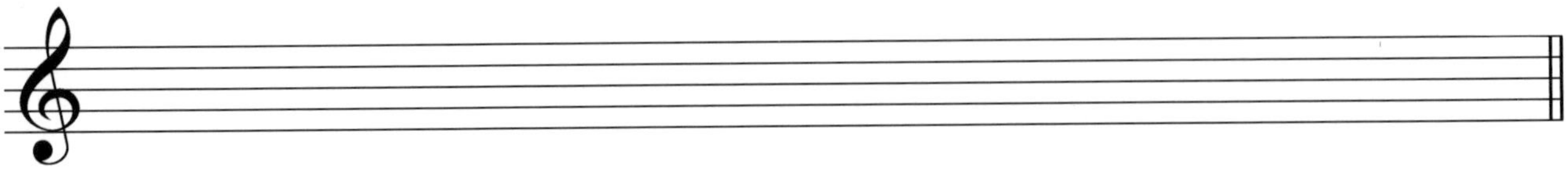

Pair up the minor key with its key signature and relative major.

C major	**D minor**	**F♯**
F major	**E minor**	No sharps or flats
G major	**A minor**	**B♭**

Harmonic Minor Scales

The harmonic minor scale is the same as the natural minor but the 7th degree is raised by one half step.

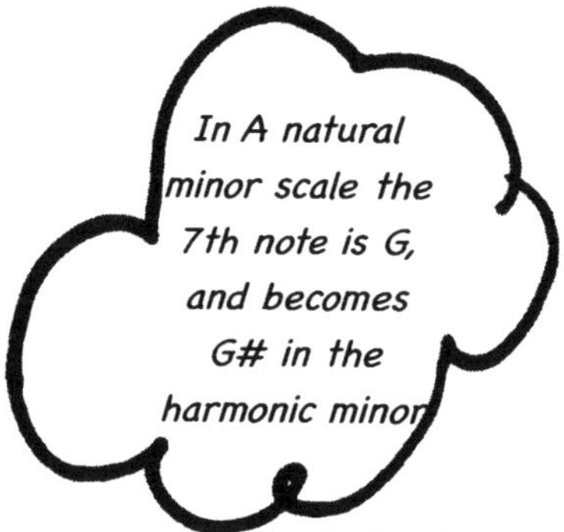
In A natural minor scale the 7th note is G, and becomes G# in the harmonic minor

Write a # by the 7th degree and complete the scale name.

.... harmonic minor scale

D harmonic .... scale

E .... minor scale

Write the A harmonic minor scale ascending and descending.

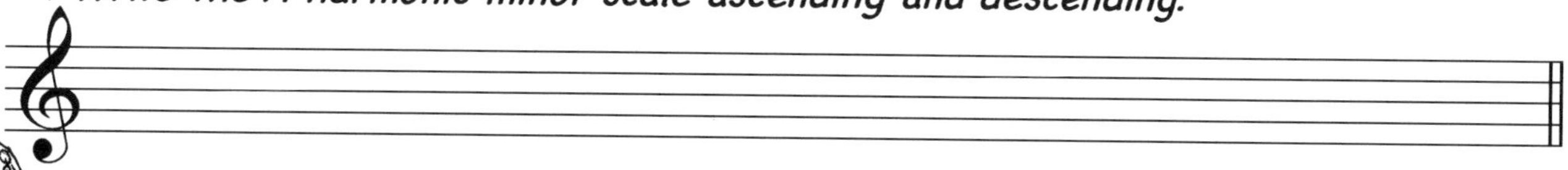

Write the D harmonic minor scale ascending and descending.

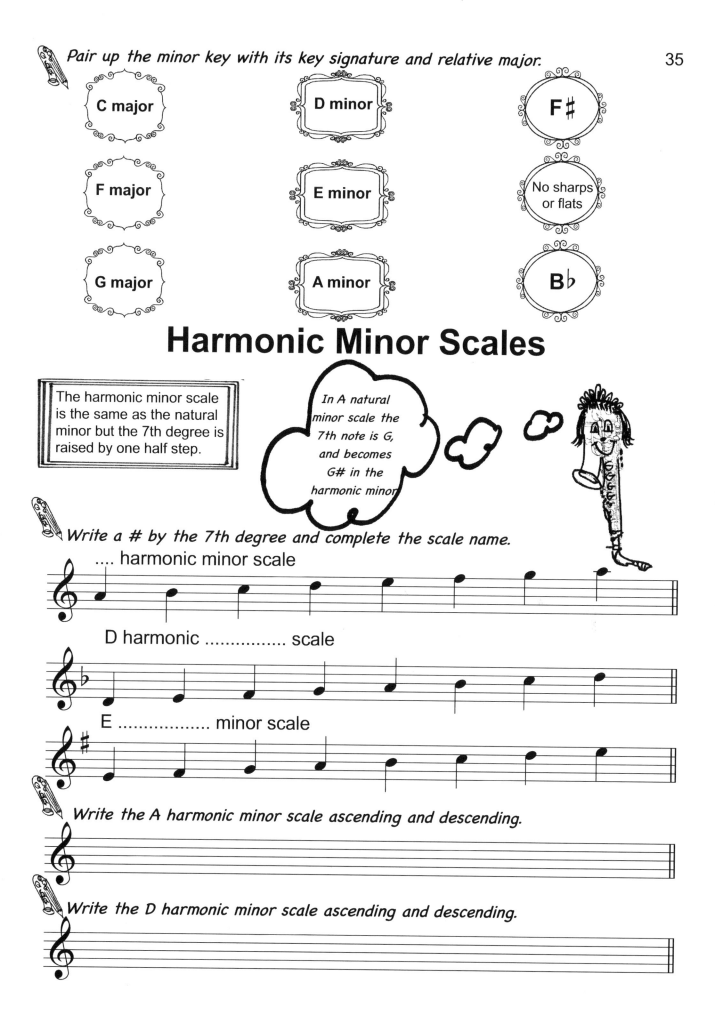

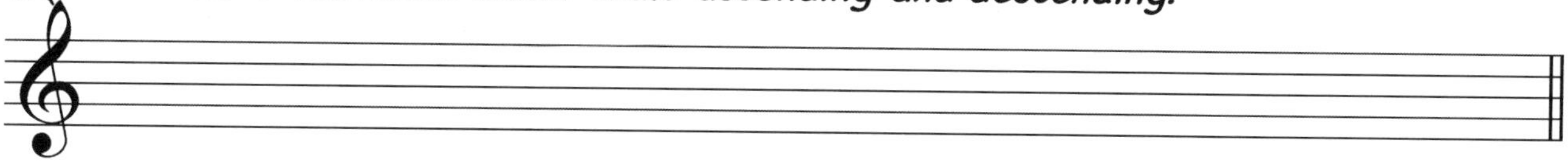

Arpeggios

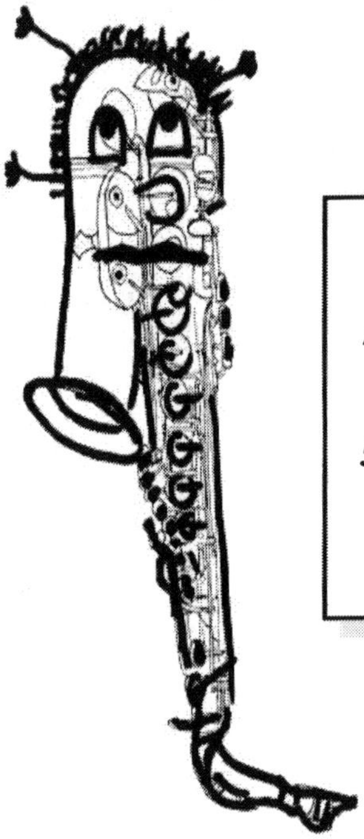

Arpeggios are made from the 1st, 3rd, 5th and 8th degrees of the scale.

Major and minor arpeggios are made in the same way.

The interval between the 1st and 3rd notes in a major scale is called a major 3rd and is made up of four half steps. In a minor scale it is called a minor 3rd and is made up of three half steps.

C major scale

① ③ ⑤ ⑧

1 2 3 4 5 6 7 8

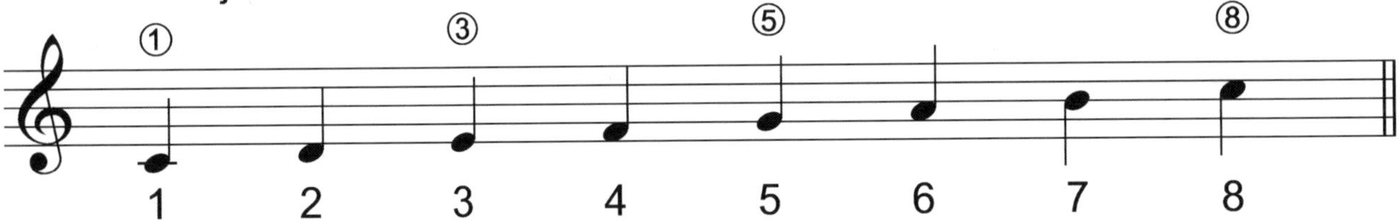

A natural minor scale

① ③ ⑤ ⑧

1 2 3 4 5 6 7 8

C major arpeggio

major third

A minor arpeggio

minor third

Colour in the notes that form the arpeggios in the scales below.

F major scale

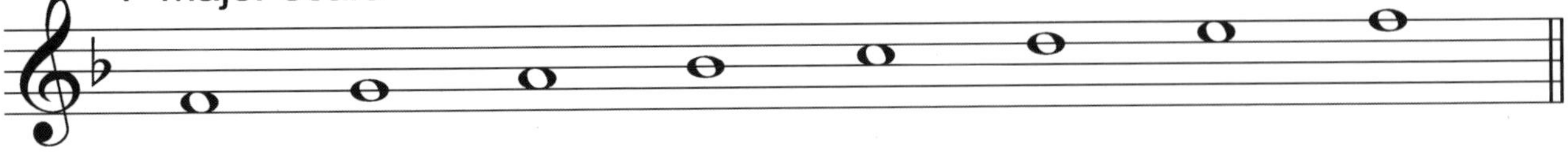

G major scale

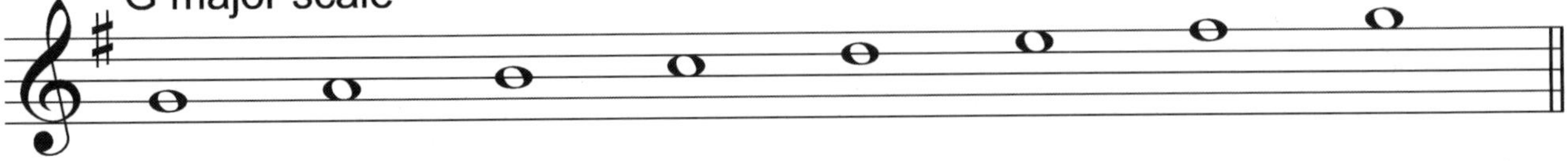

Remember to count from the lowest note of the scale.

Colour in the notes that form the arpeggios in the scales below.

C major scale

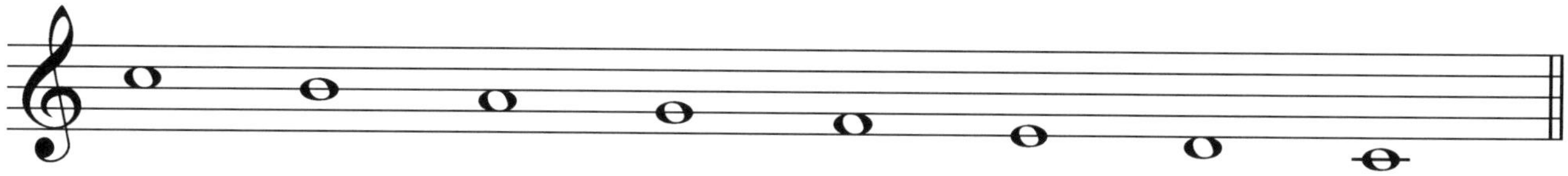

D natural minor scale

Write the arpeggio with its key signature. Use any note value.

F major

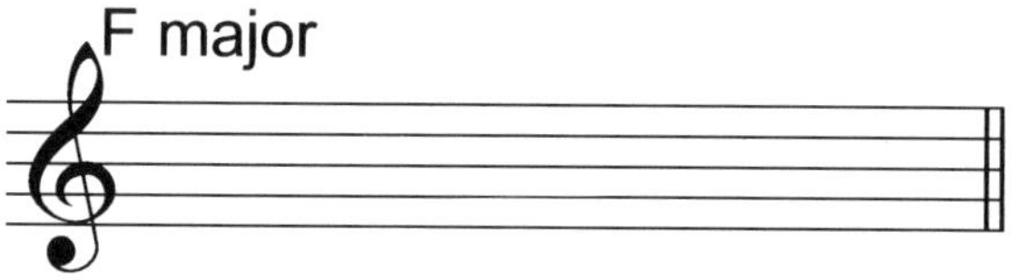

D minor

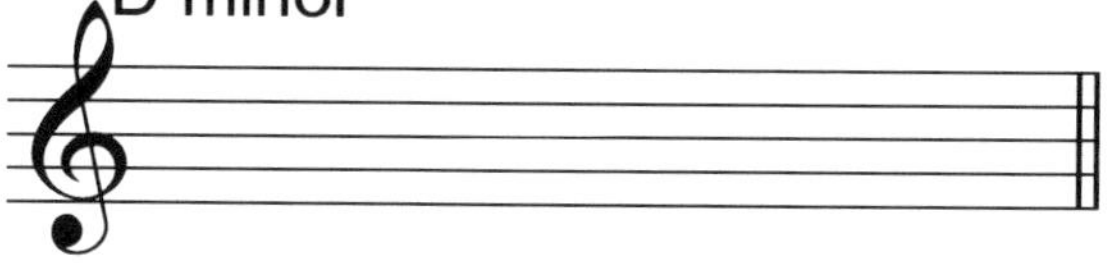

G major

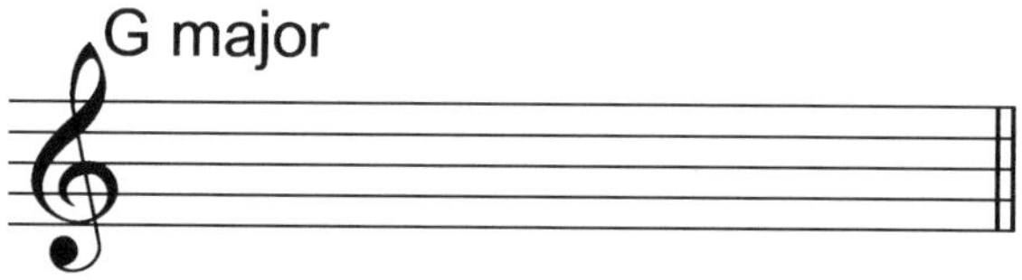

E minor

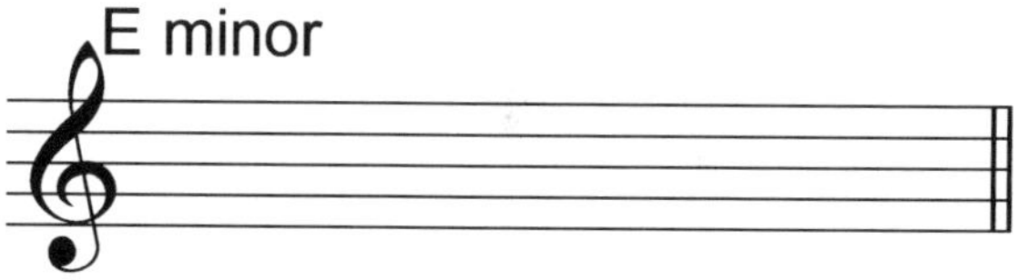

Write a phrase using only the notes from F major arpeggio.

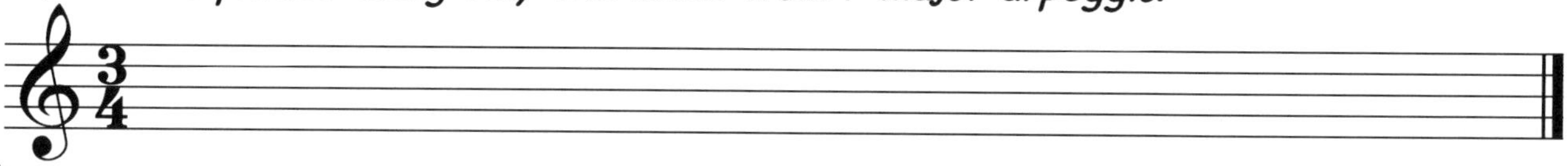

Write a phrase using only the notes from A minor arpeggio.

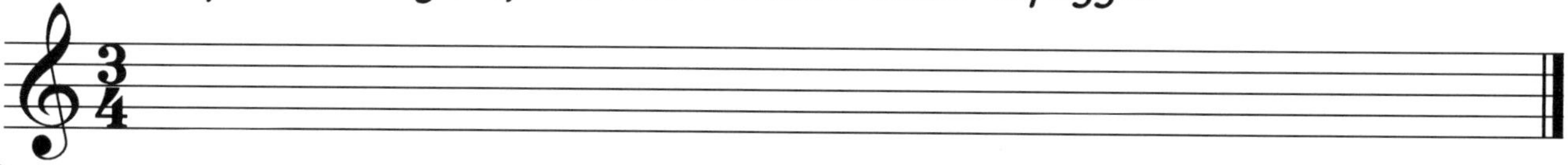

Write a phrase using only the notes from G major arpeggio.

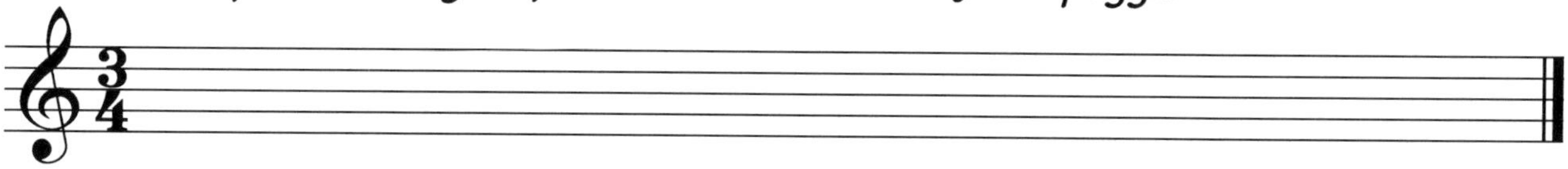

Dorian Scales

Originally one of the ancient Greek modes, the Dorian scale is formed on the second note of the major scale.

A long time before musicians began thinking about keys, there were types of scales called modes.

The Dorian mode is similar to the natural minor scale except for the sixth note.

Examples of songs using the Dorian mode are: 'Horse With No Name' and 'Mad World'.

Dorian scale on D (in C) (ascending)

Dorian scale on G (in F) (ascending)

Write the missing notes in this dorian scale.

Write the dorian scale on D descending.

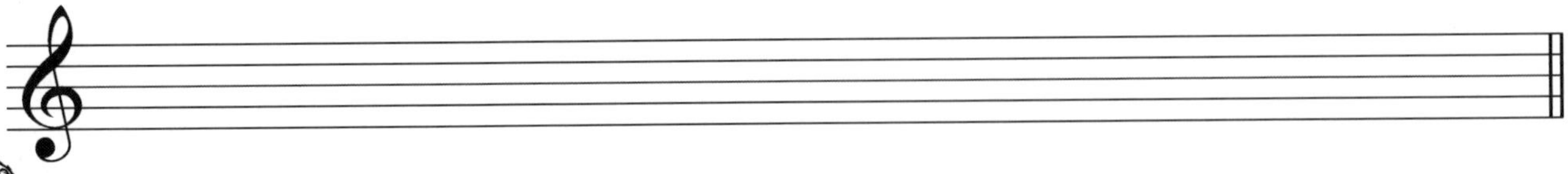

Write a phrase using only the notes from the Dorian scale on G and then play it.

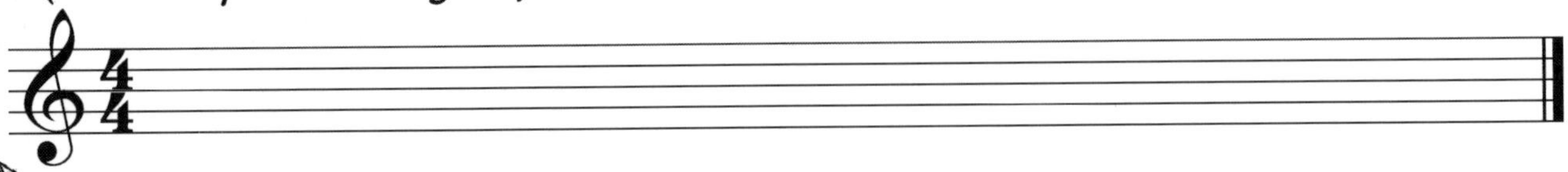

Write a phrase using only the notes from the Dorian scale on D and then play it.

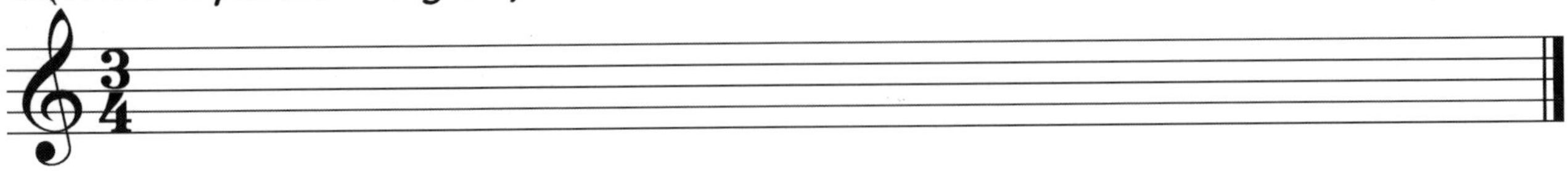

Mixolydian Scales

The ancient Greek modes were named after different regions of Greece.

The Seven Greek Modes are:
Ionian
Dorian
Phrygian
Lydian
Mixolydian
Aeolian
Locrian

The Mixolydian scale is also, originally, one of the ancient Greek modes, and is formed on the fifth note of the major scale.

Examples of songs using the Mixolydian mode are: 'Sweet Home Alabama' and 'Norwegian Wood'..

The main survivors from the seven ancient Greek modes are the Ionian (now called the major scale) and the Aeolian (minor scale) .

Mixolydian scale on G (in C) (ascending)

Mixolydian scale on D (in G) (ascending)

Write the missing notes in this moxolydian scale.

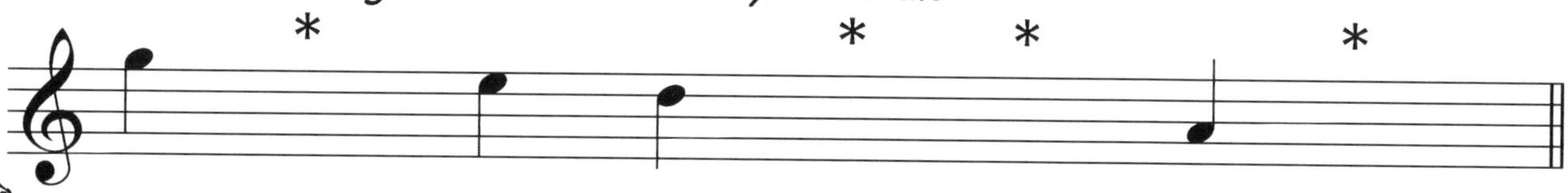

Write a phrase using only the notes from the Dorian scale on G and then play it.

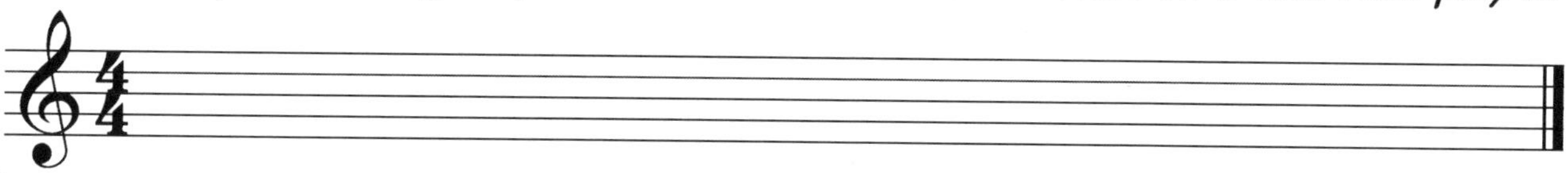

Write a phrase using only the notes from the Dorian scale on D and then play it.

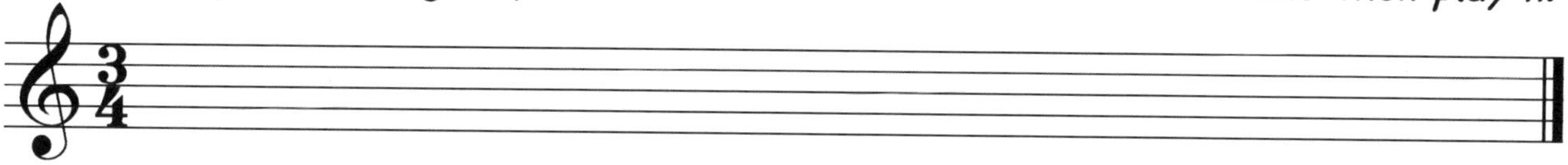

Check 4 How much do you remember?

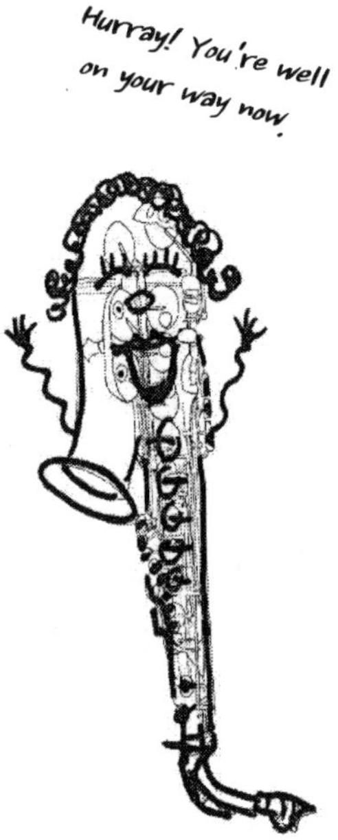

Mix and Match

Match the scale with its key signature.

A minor scale	F♯
E minor scale	B♭
D minor scale	No ♯ No ♭

Quick Check

Are the arpeggios correct? Tick or cross them.

A minor arpeggio *G major arpeggio* *F major arpeggio*

Quiz

True or false? Circle the right answer.

1. A natural minor scale has exactly the same notes as C major scale. True False
2. An octopus is an interval of eight notes. True False
3. Each minor scale shares a key signature with a major scale. True False
4. Arpeggios are made from the 1st, 3rd, 5th and 7th notes of a scale. True False
5. D minor and F major share a key signature. True False

How many did you get right? ☐

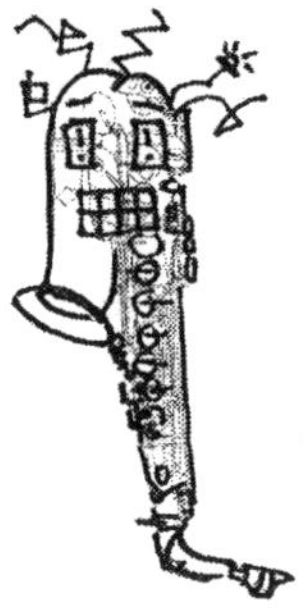

Musical Symbols

In music, symbols are used to show musical detail e.g. whether to play loud or quiet (dynamics) or how to tongue (articulation) and many others. Here are a few of the most commonly used.

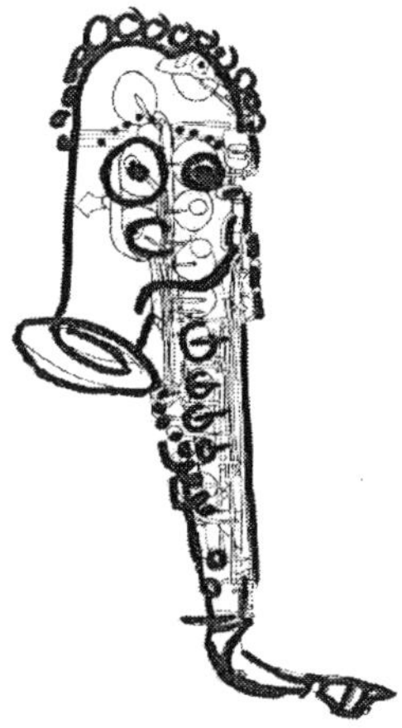

 *gradually louder*

 *gradually quieter*

’ *Breath Mark (sometimes* ∨ *or* ✓ *are used instead)*

Slur -joined smoothly

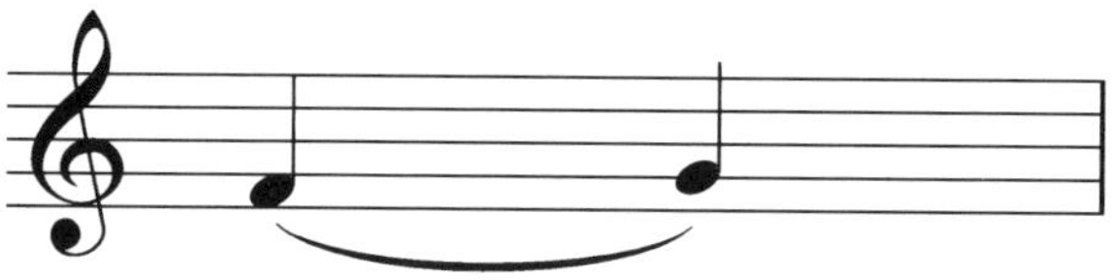

Fermata - pause on the note

Phrase mark - showing one musical phrase

Accent - stressed strongly

Staccato - short, detached

Tenuto - held and given a slight pressure

Trill- alternate rapidly to the note above

Musical Terms

Italian words are often used in music to show tempo (speed), dynamics (louds and softs) and directions. Many of them are abbreviated. Here are some of the most commonly used.

accelerando / accel. - *gradually faster*
adagio - *slow*
allegretto - *fairly fast (but not as fast as allegro)*
allegro - *fast*
andante - *at a medium (walking) speed*
crescendo / cresc. - *gradually louder*
da capo / D.C. - *repeat from the beginning*
dal segno / D.S. - *repeat from the sign*
decrescendo / decresc. - *gradually quieter*
diminuendo / dim. - *gradually quieter*
dolce - *sweetly*
fine - *the end*
f **forte** - *loud*
ff **fortissimo** - *very loud*
grazioso - *graceful*
largo - *slow, stately*
legato - *smoothly*
mezzo - *moderately*
mf **/ mezzo forte** - *moderately loud*
mp **/ mezzo piano** - *moderately quiet*
moderato - *moderately*
p **/ piano** - *quiet*
pp **/ pianissimo** - *very quiet*
presto - *fast*
rallentando / rall. - *gradually slower*
ritenuto / rit. - *held back*
tempo - *speed, time (**a tempo** - in time)*
vivace - *lively, fast*

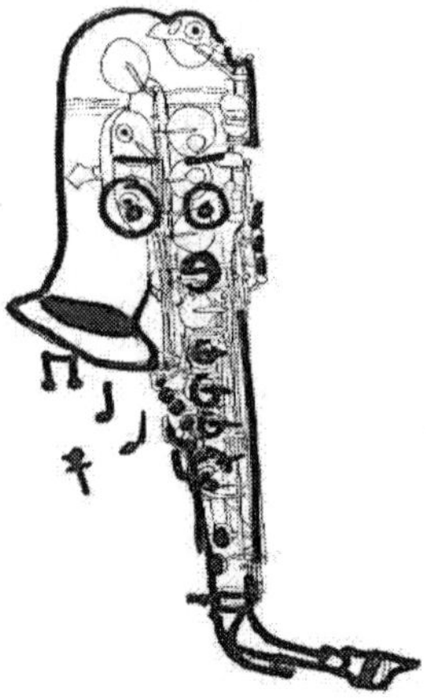

Metronome Marking

♩ = **76** *76 quarter notes in a minute*

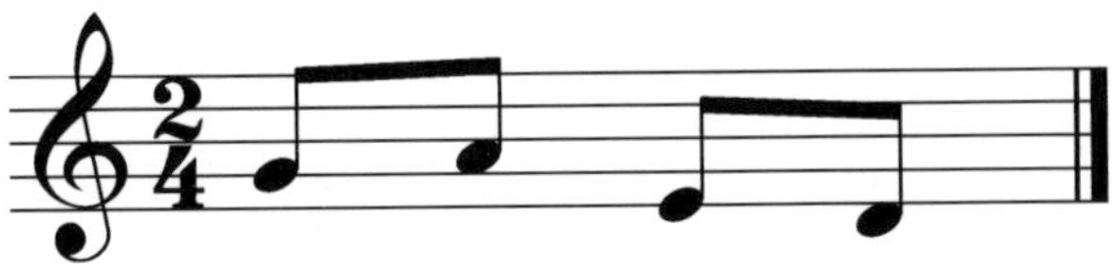

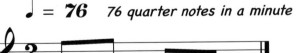

Swing Time

Pairs of eighth notes are played 'long - short'

Rearrange these dynamic markings from quietest to loudest.

p ***f*** ***mf*** ***ff*** ***pp*** ***mp***

....

Join the term, abbreviation and symbol to its description.

rallentando

cresc.

accel.

diminuendo

gradually quieter

gradually louder

gradually slower

gradually faster

crescendo

rall.

accelerando

dim.

Write the symbol.

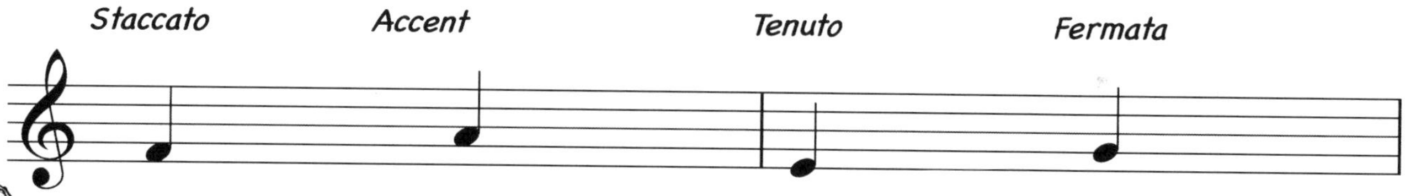

Add symbols and dynamics to this phrase of music. Be as creative as you like!

Write a phrase that changes tempo gradually.

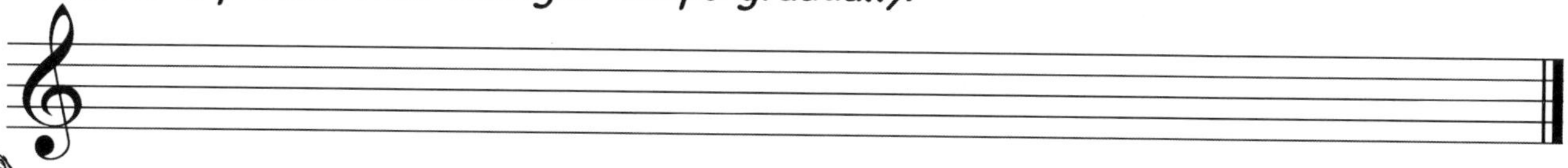

Write a phrase that changes dynamic gradually.

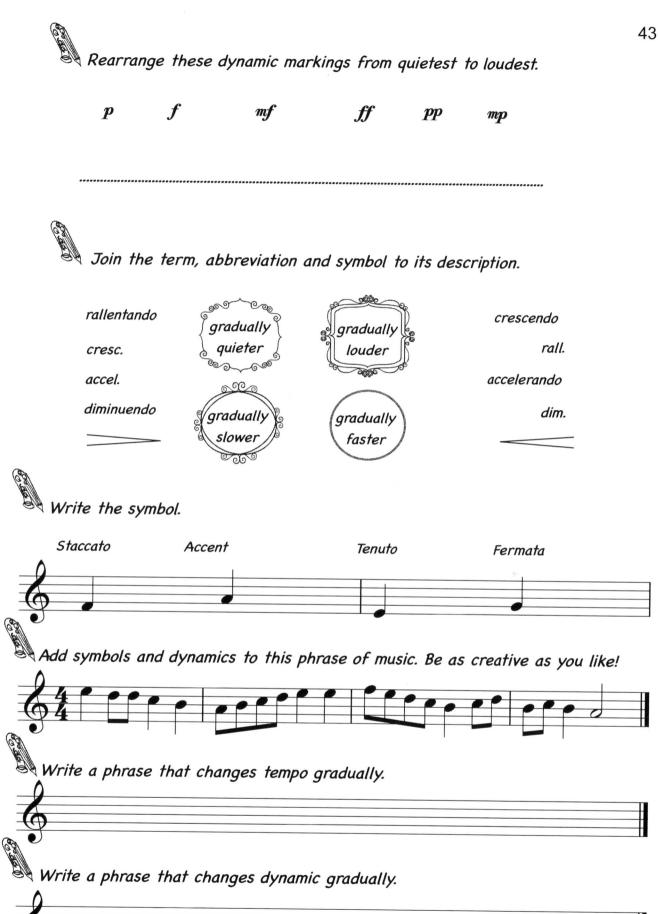

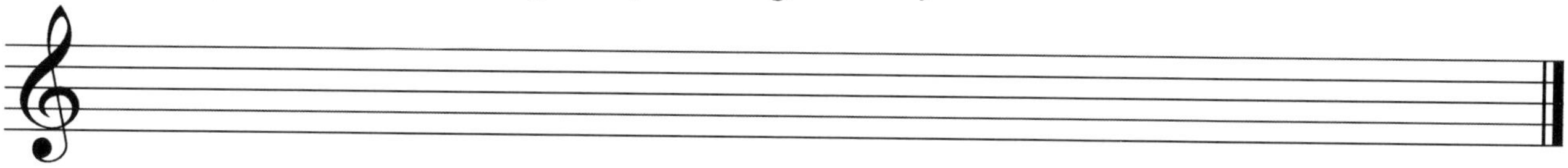

Repeats and Directions

Repeat from the beginning

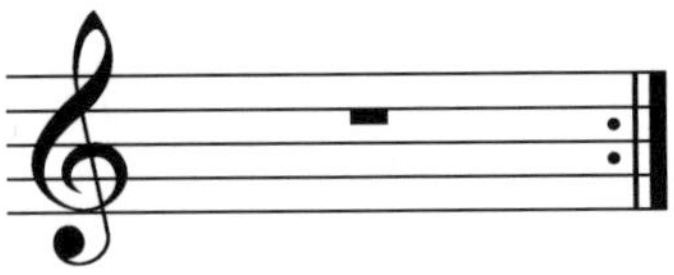

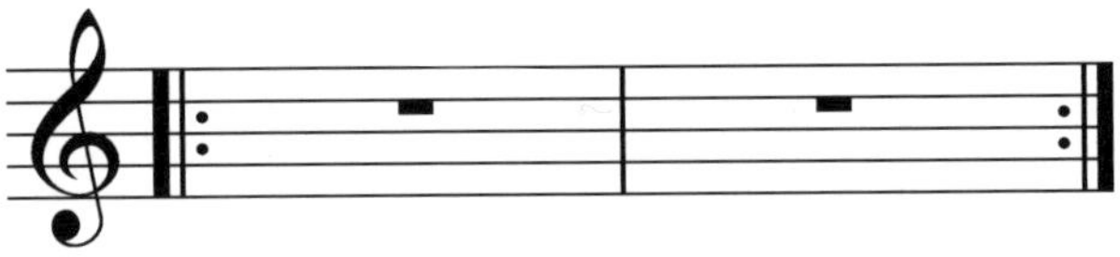

Repeat the section

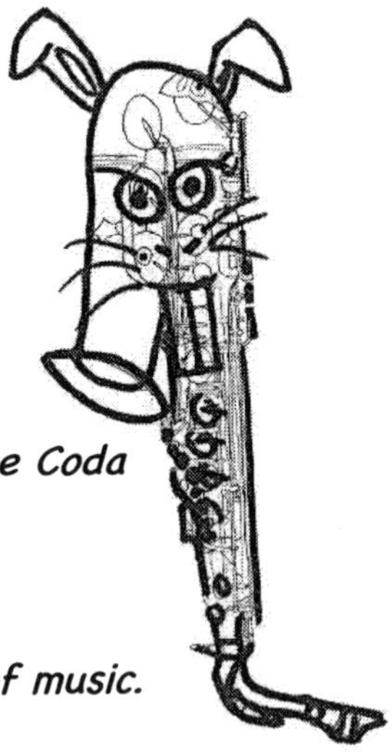

D.S.	*Dal Segno*	*Repeat from the sign*
𝄋	*Segno*	*Sign*
D.S. al Coda		*Repeat from the sign and then play the Coda*
𝄌	*Coda*	*A coda is a phrase that ends a piece of music.*
D.C.	*Da Capo*	*Go back to the beginning*
D.C. al Fine		*Go back to the beginning and play to Fine*

First-time Bars and Second-time Bars

When a composer wants a tune to be repeated but with a different ending the second time, he or she might use First-time Bars and Second-time Bars instead of writing out the tune in full.

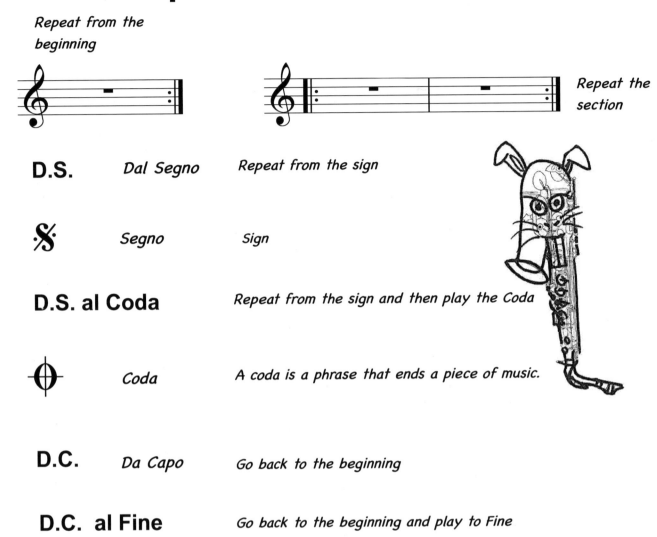

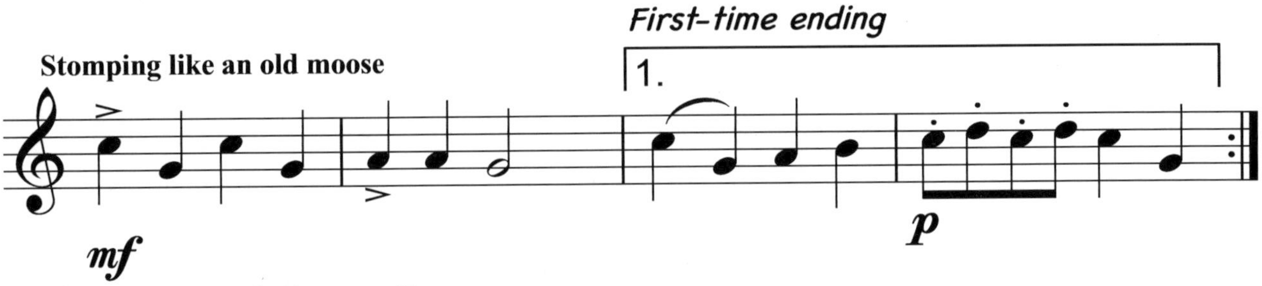

Create a trail. Draw arrows to show where you go and explain the dynamic markings in this piece.

Dizzy Demon

from our Demon Studies book

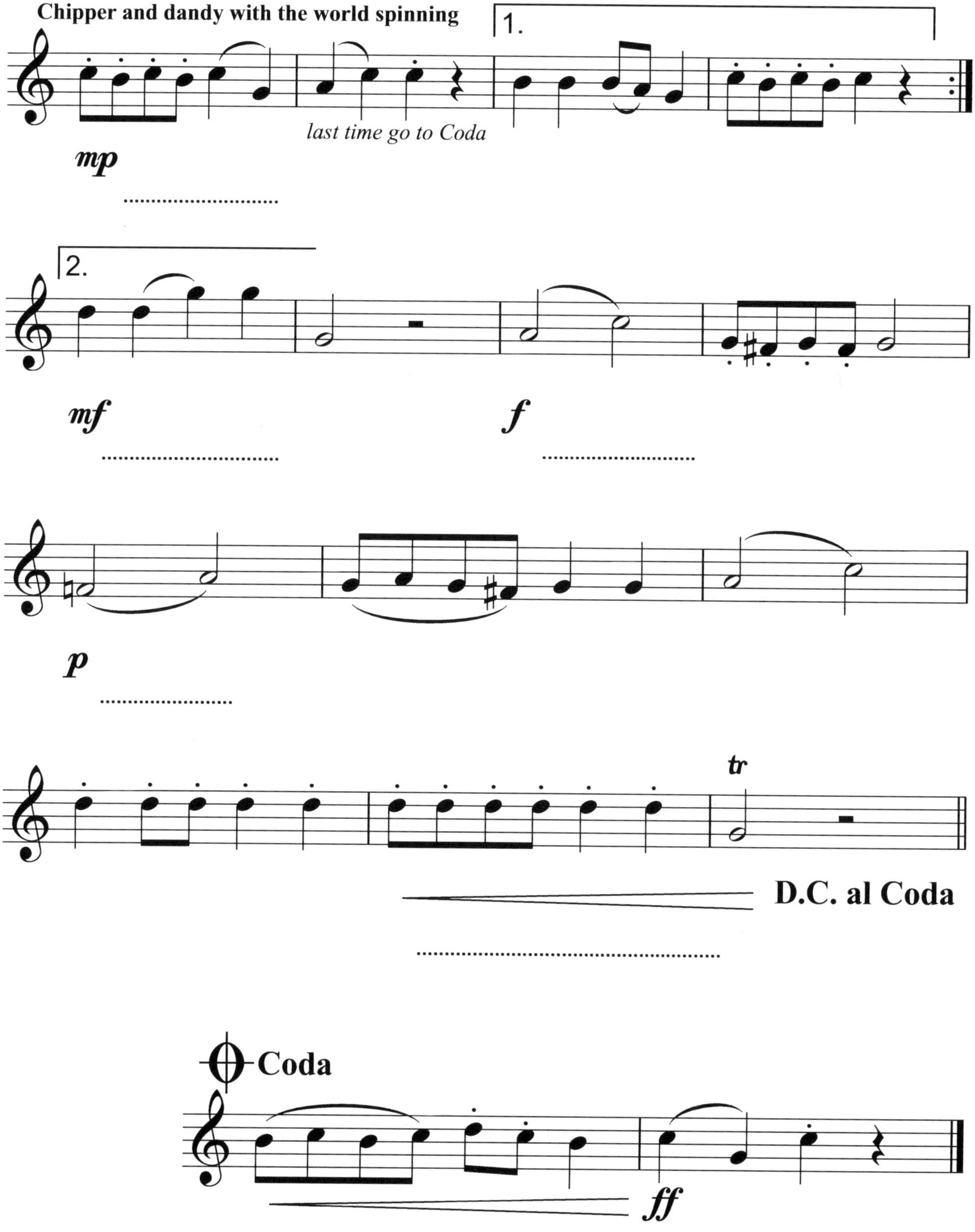

Transposing

A transposing instrument is an instrument whose music is written at a pitch that's different from the pitch that actually sounds.

Transposing instruments include: saxophone, clarinet, piccolo, cor anglais, trumpet, basset horn and French horn.

The saxophone is a transposing instrument. The alto and baritone saxophones are in Eb and the soprano and tenor saxophones are n Bb.

Instruments that are at concert pitch (where the written note is the same as the sound) include: flute, oboe, bassoon, violin, cello, piano, harp and many more.

Alto sax music is written a 6th higher than it sounds. Tenor sax music is written a 9th higher (an octave plus one).

1 Written for Tenor Sax in Bb.

2 Written for Alto Sax in Eb.

If a tenor sax plays example 1 and an alto sax plays example 2 and a flute or piano plays example 3, they will all sound at the same pitch.

3 Actually sounding (concert pitch).

Join the instrument to its description.

Concert Pitch

Transposing

If these notes are played on the alto sax (in E flat), write in the letternames of the actual sound - a sixth lower.

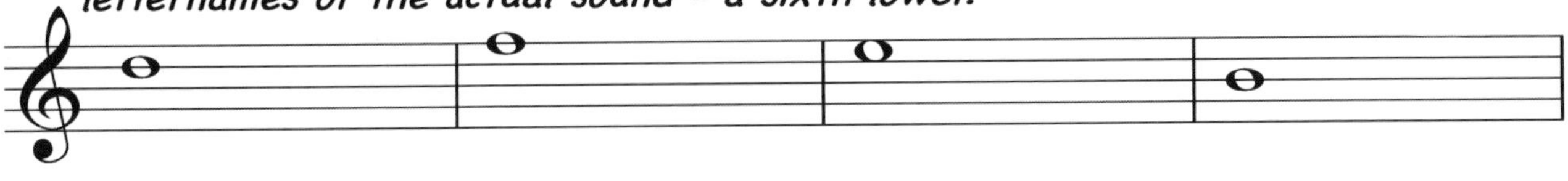

....

Check 5 How much do you remember?

Fantastic work! You've nearly finished. What a mover!

Mix and Match
Match the term with its definition.

D.S.	moderately loud
D.C.	gradually faster
pp	gradually quieter
mf	gradually slower
Allegro	at a medium (walking) speed
Andante	gradually louder
diminuendo	repeat from the beginning
crescendo	very quiet
rallentando	repeat from the sign
accelerando	quick

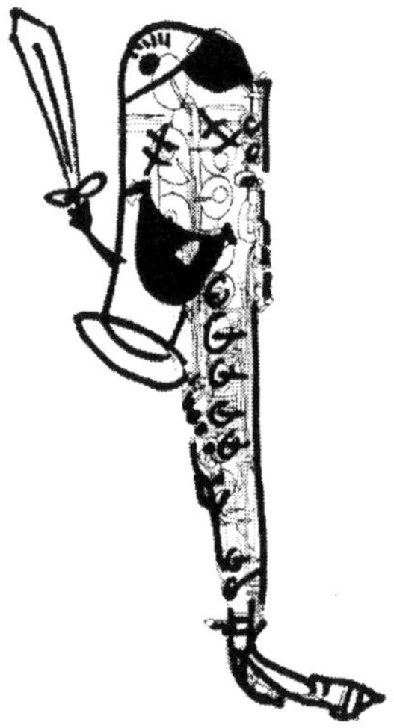

Quick Check
Are the symbols correct? Tick or cross them.

Quiz
True or false? Circle the right answer.

1. D.C. means go back to the sign. True False
2. Trills move from the written note to the note below. True False
3. ***Fine*** means 'the beginning'. True False
4. An accent is shown by a little arrow. True False
5. A staccato note is shown by a dot. True False
6. First and Second-time Bars are different endings. True False
7. D.S. means go back to the begining. True False
8. A saxophone's C sounds the same as a flute's C. True False

How many did you get right? ☐

The Saxophone

How well do you know your saxophone?

Draw arrows to the parts of the saxophone.

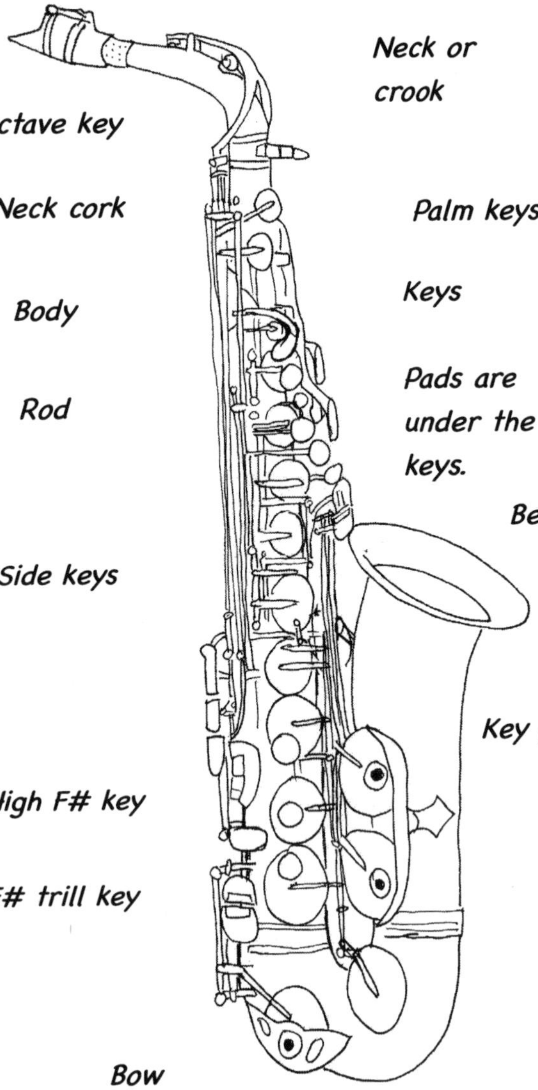
Ligature
Reed
Mouthpiece
Neck or crook
Octave key
Neck cork
Palm keys
Keys
Body
Pads are under the keys.
Rod
Bell
Side keys
Key guard
High F# key
F# trill key
Bow
Tone hole

Caring for Your Saxophone

Take care of the octave key when you assemble the saxophone. Use a gentle pushing and twisting action. Sticky drinks can cause sticky pads, so don't eat or drink before playing. After playing, swab the neck using a neck brush inserted from the wider metal end, and the body (from bell to top) using a soft cotton pull-through cloth. This will extend the life of the pads. Don't forget that germs can gather in a mouthpiece. Remove the reed and ligature and brush through or clean the mouthpiece after each playing session, rinse with lukewarm water if necessary.

Smear cork grease on the neck cork if it is dry.

Wipe fingerprints and oils from the body with a soft cloth.

The Range of the Saxophone (as written)

The Saxophone Family

There are four principal members of the saxophone family.

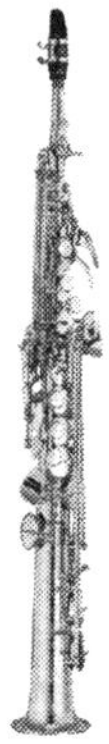

Soprano Saxophone in Bb (can also be curved)

Alto Saxophone in Eb

Tenor Saxophone in Bb

Baritone Saxophone in Eb

The biggest saxophone is the Subcontrabass Saxophone which is in Bb, over 2 metres tall and very rare.

Contrabass Saxophone in Eb 1.9 metres tall

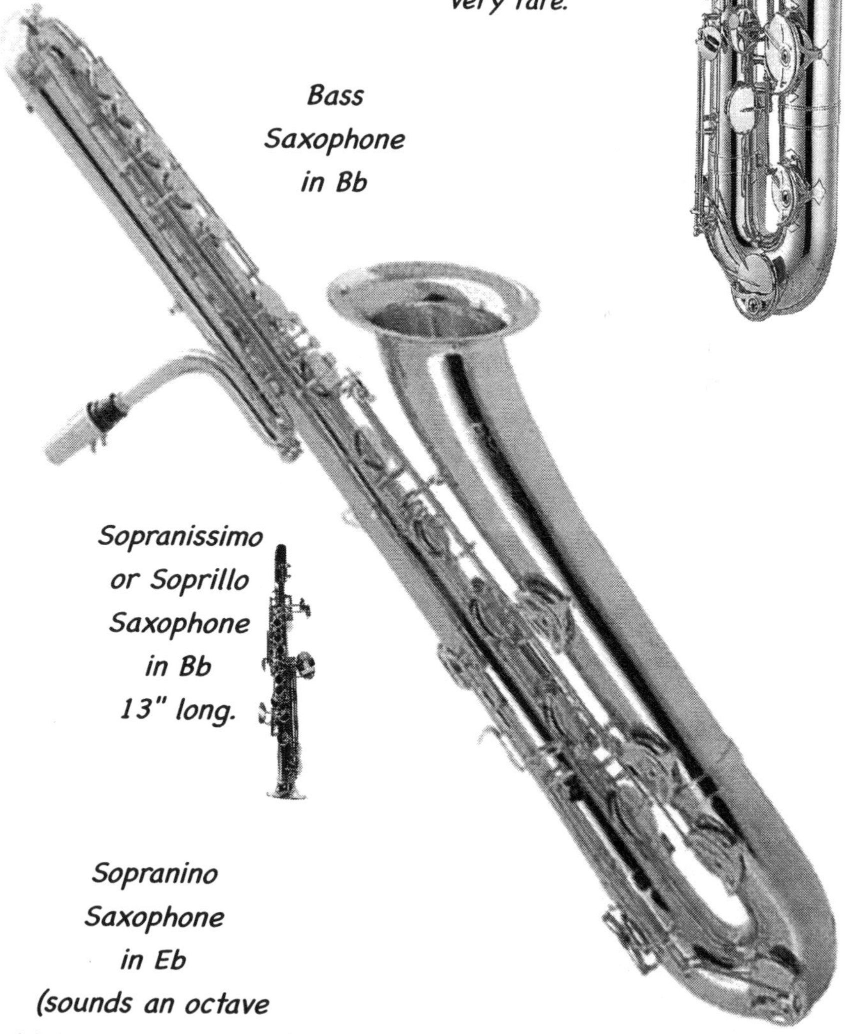

Bass Saxophone in Bb

Sopranissimo or Soprillo Saxophone in Bb 13" long.

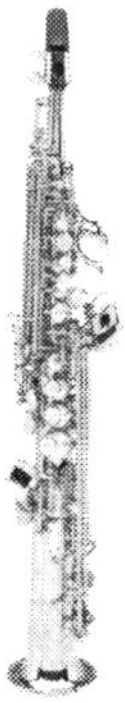

Sopranino Saxophone in Eb (sounds an octave higher than the alto)

The Woodwind Family

The saxophone is a member of the woodwind family. This is because, like the clarinet, a reed is used to produce the sound.

Circle the instrument that is not a member of the woodwind family.

Flute

Piccolo

Clarinet

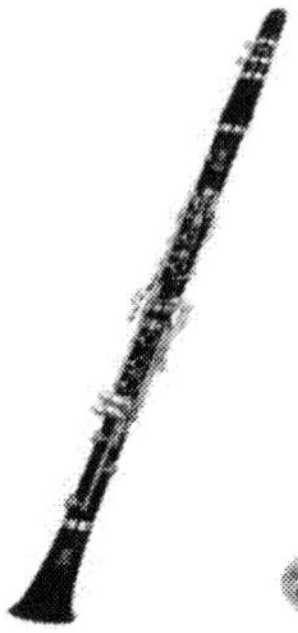

Bass Clarinet

Oboe

Cor Anglais

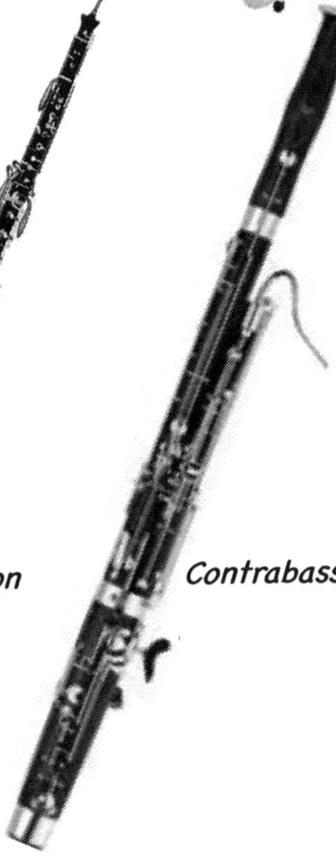

Saxophone

Bassoon

Contrabassoon

Trumpet

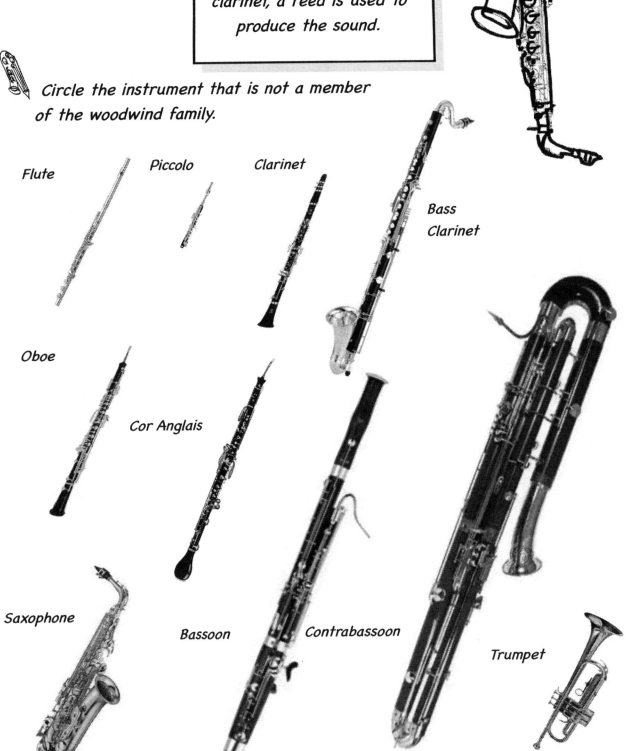

Interesting Saxophone Facts

The saxophone was invented in 1846 by Adolphe Sax, a Beligian instrument maker.

The saxophone is a 'single reed' instrument because it plays on one piece of reed, like the clarinet. Oboes and bassoons use double reeds that are made out of two pieces of reed.

When he invented the saxophone, Adolphe Sax wanted to make an instrument as loud as a brass instrument but as agile as a woodwind instrument.

Reeds are made from a sort of grass called Arundo Donax that grows in the Mediterranean parts of France and Spain and in California.

The brass body of the saxophone is coated with acrylic lacquer or silver plate to protect the brass from rusting.

Before the saxophone became the iconic jazz instrument of the 20th century, it was played in military bands and dance bands.

Saxophones are usually made from brass (70% copper and 30% zinc) but other materials have been used such as bronze, plastic, copper alloys, silver and even wood.

To showcase his new instrument, Adolphe Sax staged a 'battle of the bands' between the French Infantry Band and his sax band. The sax band won!

During the 'sax craze' of the early 1900s several American cities banned the saxophone from being played on the streets between the hours of 10pm and dawn.

Famous orchestral pieces with saxophone include: Ravel's 'Bolero', Rachmaninov's 'Symphonic Dances', Mussorgsky's 'Pictures at an Exhibition'.

Tom Selleck (actor), Kesha (singer), Alan Davie (artist), Bob Dylan (singer), Herol Graham (boxer), David Bowie (singer), Lionel Richie (singer), Jennifer Garner (actor), Jude Law (actor) Dolly Parton (singer), Rainn Wilson (actor), Gary Stevens (footballer), Bill Clinton (U.S. president), and Zoot (muppet), all played the saxophone.

Most student mouthpieces are made from plastic. Metal mouthpieces make a more powerful sound but hard rubber mouthpieces are also in use. Mouthpieces were originally made from wood. Mouthpieces have also been made from glass, bone, and porcelain.

The longest note played on a saxophone lasted for over an hour and a half and was played by Geovanny Escalante who used circular breathing.

Rico reeds are made with pressed cane. Vandorens use solid cane.

Final Check

Wordsearch

Can you find these words?

C	D	H	Y	A	N	D	A	N	T	E	K	I	M	D
O	D	N	E	C	S	E	R	C	P	T	T	P	E	L
C	K	G	R	A	Z	I	O	S	O	E	G	C	O	T
A	O	F	S	E	V	Z	K	T	N	O	R	M	T	V
B	K	D	C	V	I	P	A	U	T	E	I	L	U	I
O	B	L	N	W	O	C	T	A	S	S	A	O	N	V
F	O	R	T	E	C	O	T	C	S	R	T	M	E	A
D	R	I	N	A	U	R	E	I	G	T	B	I	T	C
A	U	X	T	A	O	N	T	O	E	E	M	S	I	E
L	L	S	J	P	D	R	I	R	W	A	G	S	R	Y
E	S	L	E	O	O	B	G	M	R	K	M	I	P	A
G	C	B	E	F	T	E	P	C	I	E	P	N	I	R
A	L	A	B	G	L	T	A	P	Z	D	J	A	A	W
T	E	S	H	L	R	T	V	Z	T	V	N	I	N	E
O	F	S	A	C	O	O	O	T	S	E	R	P	O	L

ALLEGRETTO
ALLEGRO
ANDANTE
BASS
CLEF
CRESCENDO
DECRESCENDO
DIMINUENDO
DOLCE
FORTE
FORTISSIMO
GRAZIOSO
LARGO
LEGATO
MEZZO
PIANO
PIANISSIMO
PRESTO
RITENUTO
SLUR
STACCATO
TENUTO
VIVACE

Congratulations! You've finished. What an achievement! Why not visit the Wild Music website and check your amswers?

Can you find these words?

ADOLPHESAX
ALTO
ARUNDODONAX
BARITONE
BELL
CONTRABASS
CORK
EMBOUCHURE
JAZZ
KEYS
LACQUER
LIGATURE
MOUTHPIECE
NECK
PADS
PALMKEYS
REED
SAXOPHONIST
SOPRANO
TENOR
WOODWIND

O A T P O S H U
M E C D F L U D G Q Z N
L E D N S Y E K U N O Y P A X D
M E M B O U C H U R E M F D P V G E D M
M O L O W S K H Y T D N I W D O O W B O S G
E R U T A G I L S Q E B R L Q T X E G U P A D S
Y S S S W X O W D Z H A Q F R A A B T B H C S B
M L J A G T V T C L S N O E S V W H X E N C A K
X D W C X J B I L A C Q U E R G P C N L U Q Q D
Z S J L U O O L H A U M H F Q I U D H L Q X S W
P Z O N A R P O S I W P T D E B V V I F U S Z C
N A Q Z H J H T S L E X C V C B A Z M A W X
A K J U K B T O O A D E I Y A O S A B S Z K
X A N O D O D N U R A Y R H P R A O G U
V M J L A Y Z I Q H I V A Z R K O O
I U U A R T Q S T Z L A T M N N
R S D S I E O T M P N F E U
Y O T Q N N K I O G C J
R E E D E O C V K P
G V Y F M R E E
S W E Z W K
N I K F
G Q

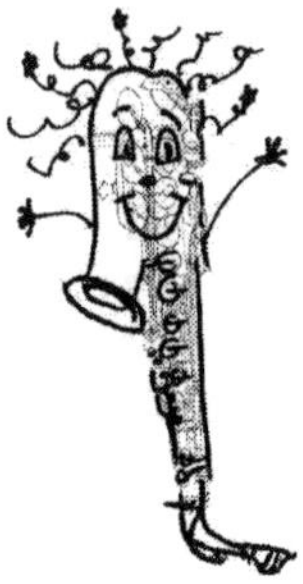

The Saxophone Player's Progress

Tick the box for each topic completed.

- [ ] Treble Clef
- [ ] Letter Names
- [ ] Note Values
- [ ] Stems
- [ ] Rests
- [ ] Check 1
- [ ] Time Signatures
- [ ] Accidentals
- [ ] Eighth Notes
- [ ] Ledger Lines
- [ ] Check 2
- [ ] Major Scales
- [ ] Key Signatures
- [ ] Dotted Quarter Notes
- [ ] Check 3
- [ ] Degrees of the Scale
- [ ] Intervals
- [ ] Minor Scales
- [ ] Arpeggios
- [ ] Dorian and Mixolydian Scales
- [ ] Check 4
- [ ] Musical Symbols
- [ ] Musical Terms
- [ ] Repeats and Directions
- [ ] Transposing
- [ ] Check 5
- [ ] The Saxophone
- [ ] The Saxophone Family
- [ ] The Woodwind Family
- [ ] Interesting Saxophone Facts
- [ ] Final Check

Congratulations

to

....

for completing

The Super Saxophone Music Theory Book 1!

If you have enjoyed **The Super Saxophone Music Theory Book 1**

why not try the other books in the **Super Saxophone** series!

For more info, please visit: **WildMusicPublications.com**

All of our books are available to download, or you can order from Amazon.

Introducing some of our favourites:

50+ Greatest Classics

Catch the Beat Sight Reading

Christmas Carols

Trick or Treat – A Halloween Suite

Intermediate Classic Duets

Fish 'n' Ships

Easy Duets from Around the World

Christmas Duets

Saxophone Music Theory Book 2

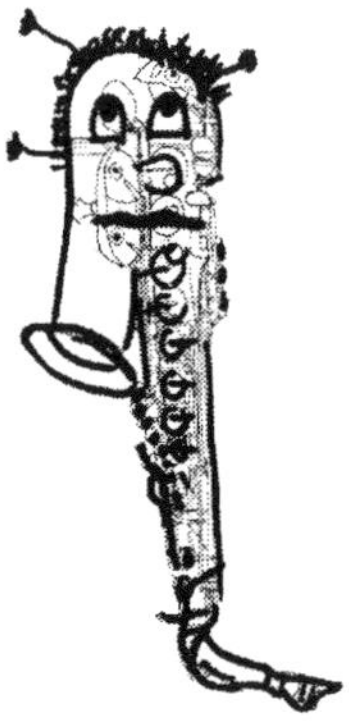

66112888R00035

Made in the USA
Middletown, DE
08 March 2018

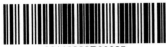